Misled

Misled

HIDDEN COLORS OF AMERICA

⌒

Roy Whitmore Ph.D.

Danielle, I hope you enjoy a peek into my life as you read Misled! Please share the history I added at the end of my book!!!
Roy Wht— 8/6/20

Copyright © 2017 Roy Whitmore Ph.D.
All rights reserved.

ISBN-13: 9781537096735
ISBN-10: 1537096737

Contents

Preface ix
Acknowledgments xiii
Introduction xv

Chapter 1   The Early Years 1
            The Sixth-Grade Horror 4
            Meeting God 5
            Sports 5
            Lesson 1: God in Your Life 6
Chapter 2   High School 8
            Class 8
            Gangbanger 9
            Mom 10
            My Vision 12
            Lesson 2: Family, Friends, and Your Life 14
Chapter 3   The Air Force 16
            Mentors, Friends, and a Test 16
            Training 18
            My First Plane Flight 19
            My Best Friend 20
            My First Mentor 20
            I Am Intelligent 22
            NCO of the Year Contest 24

	Diversity Training	25
	Life for Me	26
	Leaving the Air Force	27
	Sears Takes Me to Red Lobster	28
	Lesson 3: Mentors and Your Life	29
Chapter 4	Target Stores	31
	Store Manager: The N Word	32
	The War Strategy vs. Walmart	33
	The Spotlight and Regional Staff	36
	District Manager	40
	Small-Market and War Strategy	43
	Regional Director and the KKK	46
	Leaving Target	49
	Class-Action Lawsuit	54
	Lesson 4: Faith in Your Life	59
Chapter 5	From Target to Jewel-Osco	61
	The Limited Corporation	62
	Jewel-Osco	62
	Keith's Promotion—and I Went South	64
	Lesson 5: Education in Your Life	66
Chapter 6	PhD Journey	69
	Global Recruiting Network (GRN)	70
	PhD Studies	71
	Lesson 6: Persistence in Life	76
Chapter 7	Our Social System	79
	Socialization Process from Childhood	79
	My Perspective	81
	The Founding Fathers' Perspective	84
	Understanding Our Founding Documents	85
	The Declaration of Independence	87
	The US Constitution	93
	Preamble	94
	Lesson 7: Your Great History	98

Chapter 8	Why Police Are Killing Black Kids · 100
	Misguided Americans · 100
	The FBI's Report · 101
	Why Some Police Shoot First · 105
	How to Change Their Cognitive Triggers · · · · · · · · · · · · · · 108
	Lesson 8: Your Social Order, Our Social System · · · · · · · · · · · 110
Chapter 9	History of Inventions and Creations: Who Really
	Made America Great? · 113
	Lesson 9: Let Your Genius Shine · 122
Chapter 10	Changing Demographic by 2050: Will You Be Ready? · · · · · 125
	History · 125
	Capitalism · 127
	Religious System · 131
	Preparing for 2050 · 132
	Lesson 10: You Can Be a Hero, Too · · · · · · · · · · · · · · · · · · · 136
Chapter 11	Reflections · 139
	Ghana · 139
	The Beginning! · 141
	Day 1 · 141
	Day 2 · 143
	Day 3 · 144
	Day 4 · 147
	Day 5 · 148
	Day 6 · 149
	Day 7 · 152
	Same-Day Reflections · 158
	Final Reflections · 159
	The End: Quotes · 161
	References · 163

Preface

IMAGINE GROWING UP IN A society that exploited you in every way conceivable. Imagine being told throughout your childhood that you had to be twice as good as a white individual to expect to earn or receive even a small portion of wealth or career success. Imagine reading from books that, in some cases, had half the pages missing. Imagine needing medical care and having doctors perform extreme procedures, such as removing teeth, removing limbs, and performing other surgical procedures, even when the medical condition did not warrant such radical treatment. Imagine watching television and constantly seeing individuals like you, African Americans, portrayed in negative and degrading positions or roles. Imagine being told by teachers that you should expect no more from life than menial jobs that offer very low wages. Imagine being black in America.

There is a misguided belief that African Americans are inferior, and there has been an attitude of general indifference toward African Americans that has caused members of the African American community to doubt themselves and their usefulness to society. These types of false beliefs have made it very challenging for African Americans to perform like others in our social system. Because of these deeply held beliefs, African Americans are held to standards that are, frankly, impossible to achieve consistently. Thus, when they fail to achieve or live up to levels that no human can achieve consistently, they were, and are, blamed for not measuring up.

African American history has not been told accurately, and often facts have been omitted that would clearly prove that African Americans have been brave soldiers in America's defense in every war, including the Revolutionary War, the War of 1812, the Mexican War, and the Civil War. So, too, African Americans have been involved in many great inventions in America, as you will learn in chapter 9. Patricia Carter Sluby, in her book *The Inventive Spirit of African Americans*, highlighted a quote from Dr. Martin Luther King Jr. that I wish to share:

> In an imaginary letter from the pen of the Apostle Paul, Dr. King wrote:
>
> I have heard so much about you and of what you are doing. News has come to me regarding the fascinating and astounding advances that you have made in the scientific realm. I have learned of your dashing subways and flashing airplanes. Through your scientific genius you have dwarfed distance and placed time in chains. You have made it possible to eat breakfast in Paris, France, and lunch in New York City. I have also heard of your skyscraper buildings with their prodigious towers rising heavenward. I am told of your great medical advances and the curing of many dread plagues and diseases, thereby prolonging your lives and offering greater security and physical wellbeing. All of that is marvelous. You can do so many things in your day that I could not do in the Greco-Roman world of my day. You travel distances in a single day that in my generation required three months. That is wonderful. What tremendous strides in the areas of scientific and technological development you have made.

King ends Paul's letter by noting that, despite all of our great achievements, we have yet to create a brotherhood by employing our greatest God-given gift as a Christian people because we have not employed our "moral and spiritual genius" to serve our brothers.

If we Americans were to situate our discussion in facts regarding black history, we would be an enlightened people, and I am convinced that much of the trouble that we currently experience in America would quickly dissipate.

For example, it would make a difference if all Americans knew that Ethiopia and Egypt led the march to civilization. Yes, they taught the Greeks, Romans, and Jews about civilization.

When I visited Accra, Ghana, I discovered the devastating facts behind the slave trade. I found that Africans were selected to be slaves because they were in better health than others, with strong, clean teeth. In fact, during the long voyage from Africa to the New World, their primary complaint was not having the capacity to clean their teeth and their bodies. They were expert craftsmen, artisans, wood-carvers, miners, toolmakers, construction workers, and artists. Africans brought these important skills to America, and they shared openly and freely.

Although it was virtually impossible for African Americans to receive any quality education in America, there were some universities that found ways to open their doors in the mid-1800s. We should all be thankful to Harvard, Walden, Rush Medical Center, and DePauw University. Also, because Washington, DC, abolished slavery in 1862, many African Americans were offered free college education in the colleges and universities located in that area.

To be clear, the intention of this work is to tell how our social system influenced me, and to offer some important information to black boys and to all of America regarding the African American male experience. Additionally, my desire is to share my view of how both African American males and our society in general can support one another intellectually, spiritually, and emotionally. I have endeavored to include supportive facts where available. Though occasionally parts of this book will challenge white males, please note that the author is clear in his understanding that not all white males have attempted to harm African Americans. In fact, to use a most disliked cliché, most of my very good friends are indeed white males. However, I believe that it is urgently important that African American males hear the lived stories of this African American and other African American males who can share lived experiences and offer positive suggestions for improvement. I think that it is important that African Americans understand how our social systems operate and how they should adjust intellectually if they are to have a positive influence on the future of our great country.

I call on all Americans to embrace the challenging issues that African American communities face with an attitude of support. Unless we intercede now, we will allow irreparable damage to our social system, our economic future, and ultimately our democracy. Remember that most African American communities did not slip into entropy on their own. America owns much of that responsibility. We, as Americans, own the poor education system, the removal of jobs, and the banking system that is restrictive to African Americans and their businesses. Yes, in a sense, many of the conditions we find in African American communities were socially and systematically constructed by us all. As such, it will take more than a neighborhood to repair the damage. It will take a country.

Finally, if we do not begin to support our African American communities with technology, coding education, and better public schools and colleges, we might see a generation of people become irrelevant, angry, and bitter. Today we have a gold mine of talent in the African American community, and we need to start mining that gold. The more intellectual ethos we mine today, the stronger America will be tomorrow. Remember that the primary reason for the beginning of the slave trade was that African labor was more valuable than gold and diamonds.

Acknowledgments

THE IDEA FOR WRITING THIS book dates back to my Target leadership days. The urge to write this book was compelling for several reasons. First, I really wished to understand why African Americans were being excluded from executive positions in Fortune 500 organizations. I did not initially believe that they were excluded due to racism because I did not wish to believe that many of the individuals I worked with were racist. In fact, even today I believe that many of my peers, supervisors, and subordinates who chose to exclude African Americans from promotions and leadership positions did so because of the structure and culture of the organizations—not because of sinister personal belief. Secondly, I think that it is urgently important that we call out organizations that have become a safe haven for individuals who practice hatred or racism. You know who you are, and you know who these individuals are within your organizations. So, too, you are aware that they practice and display racism and biased behaviors toward minorities. Finally, I wanted to give all men, in particular African American boys and men, a document that they can relate to—a document that can offer them help and hope today, not years from now.

I can say today that this writing has served to help me grow in many different ways. I have become a more enlightened person with a much deeper appreciation for those I encounter and engage each day. This writing has helped me to become what I believe to be the real Roy Whitmore.

It is with deep gratitude that I thank my wife, Dot, my greatest supporter, love, and friend. It has, indeed, been a challenging last few years as I worked on this book, did consulting, and led a business school. In many ways this is a shared accomplishment, one that she accomplished equally. Finally, thanks to Dr. Mohammed Miah for his suggestion of the title.

Introduction

> I am not interested in picking up crumbs of compassion thrown from the table of someone who considers himself my master. I want the full menu of human rights.
>
> —Desmond Tutu

> Section 1. All persons born or naturalized in the United States, and subject to the jurisdiction thereof, are citizens of the United States and of the State wherein they reside. No State shall make or enforce any law which shall abridge the privileges or immunities of citizens of the United States; nor shall any State deprive any person of life, liberty, or property, without due process of law; nor deny to any person within its jurisdiction the equal protection of the laws.
>
> —The US Constitution, Amendment XIV, Section 1

Before I became a Regional Director for Target stores, and later Jewel-Osco, I was very much aware that our talent selection process was biased, but I did not understand how the system was used to exclude some talent, while including others that were, oftentimes, not deserving of a promotion or a management position. However, I quickly learned the code words that the executives used to exclude, most often, African American males. As I reflect now, I can see that their approach to excluding African Americans was obvious and systematic.

During the interview process for external or internal African American candidates, in virtually every case, they were labeled as not being perceptive or not having the capacity to see the big picture. I am sure that if one could uncover old interviewing documents at Target stores, they could easily confirm this fact. However, at that time, I knew African Americans were being excluded, but I could not really explain why. In fact, I did not understand what they meant by "lacking perception" or that an individual "could not see the big picture." However, I pretended to know, lest they label me as missing the big picture also. Occasionally I asked the executives involved in the interviewing process to explain their meaning to me, and they would respond, "You know, they are just not a good fit." This process of open discrimination drove me to learn more, and I would only obtain complete clarity as I completed my first master's degree at DePaul University. Understanding what was occurring during those interviews also drove me to gain a deeper understanding of how senior executives selected their senior-level direct reports. As a result, I dedicated my dissertation during my PhD studies to this subject. Thus, in a sense, this book represents some of my documented findings.

This volume attempts to place into context and to connect our social system, capitalistic system, and religious system, and to some degree our legal and justice systems, in such a manner that black boys, and all people, can better understand how our various systems influence and affect our behavior. If one does not understand the various systems that control America, navigating the complexities of our great society is virtually impossible.

To put this tome into perspective, it is not intended to be a scholarship of human behavior, though I do seek to support much of the conversation with data—with the exception of my personal experience, which I feel is invaluable to the audience such that they can connect my experiences with their personal experiences. So, too, I offer suggestions that can be implemented in one's life right away, suggestions that will improve the lives of the readers.

This book seeks to build confidence in black boys throughout the world, but particularly here in America. Additionally, I am hopeful that all Americans will learn much about one another as they read through this writing, and ultimately come to embrace one another with dignity, respect, and love. I have defended some of the fine police in America, because I do believe that most of our police have intentions to serve and protect us just as they swore to do. However, there are a few who should be removed, so that our police and African American communities can come together in support of one another.

Finally, some facts that African Americans should be proud of include these:

- African Americans own 2.6 million businesses, and the number is increasing.
- There are six hundred fifty thousand black-owned firms.
- There are 2.2 million black military veterans.
- Eighty-four point four percent of blacks age twenty-five and over have high school diplomas or higher.
- Twenty percent of blacks age twenty-five and over have a bachelor's degree or higher.
- One point eight million blacks age twenty-five and over have advanced degrees.
- Eighty-eight point two percent of blacks are covered by health insurance, as compared to 89.6 percent overall nationally.
- African Americans have a $35,398 annual median household income, as compared to $53,657 nationally.
- Fifty percent of blacks are married.
- Twenty-eight point six percent of civilian-employed blacks age sixteen and over have worked in management, business, science, and the arts, as compared to 36.9 percent of the total population.
- Seventeen point eight million eligible blacks voted in the 2012 election—a higher percentage of their population than white voters.

You must vote, please. Remember: "Section 1. The right of citizens of the United States to vote shall not be denied or abridged by the United States or by any State on account of race, color, or previous condition of servitude" (US Constitution, Amendment XV, Section 1).

CHAPTER 1

The Early Years

I WAS BORN TO MARY Emma (Goode) Whitmore in John Gaston Hospital in Memphis, Tennessee. To a great degree, the early years of my life shaped my view of the world. Not unlike many African American families during that time and even today, we had little in terms of capital, food, or housing. I can vaguely recall seeing the ground through the holes in the raggedy wooden floors of an old, broken-down house that we shared with cousins for a short period when living in what we considered the country—Raleigh, Tennessee. We eventually moved to a community in North Memphis across the track from the more affluent section named Douglass. This is where my worldview began to form.

My early memories as a child, until I was maybe six or seven, are somewhat blurred, but I recall that on many occasions, my mom would leave me with an Italian family, and they would treat me as if I were the king of the house, feeding me wonderful Italian foods—mostly pasta. In fact, they cared so much for me that they would hide me or pretend that I was asleep when my mom came to pick me up, and I would have the opportunity to live a better life for a short while longer. Even today, my love for pasta continues. It was during these critical developmental years that I came to better understand how life was different for some people, better for others and even worse for some as they sought equality and financial freedom in our great country.

Though at the time I did not understand the meaning of race—I did not understand how being of a different skin color was a reason for others to treat me differently—I was destined to learn, just as all African Americans have been shamefully forced to learn. Later, during my educational process at DePaul University, I began to learn the socially constructed reasons why some were left behind. I also learned that there are no scientific reasons for America, and the world, to be misled about the rich history of African Americans. In fact, most of the lies about African Americans were paraded as facts because of the desire to grow capital here in America.

The utter craziness of this myth is that many whites really believe the lies that were told about African Americans, and the sad part of this horror story is that many African Americans have come to believe the fabricated lies about our past, too. Far too many actually live out the behaviors as created by others—behaviors that strip them of their dignity, courage, creativity, and worst of all, love for family and race. I am thankful that through my educational process, I learned the many reasons why finding success of any kind in areas other than music, sports, or common labor in life was virtually impossible for some but oftentimes given as a privileged right to others—even when they were not successful or educated. I also discovered that African Americans had far more to do with the success of America than was ever explained in our history books. I can't help but wonder what or where most African Americans would be today financially if we had access to quality education before the 1950s and if our history as told to all Americans had been facts, not lies.

It was during my critical, formative years that I developed a strong self-confidence while I lived consistently with an Italian family—a confidence that was shattered when I entered the first grade at Douglass School in North Memphis. It was there that I first encountered the powerful African American socialization process in action—a process that would prove to be destructive to me, an African American child. It is there that I was forced to believe that I was less than whites, and even less than human. As I reflect, I now realize that teachers of color were the anointed masters of our socialization process, and that is heartbreaking indeed. I also understand how uneducated most of these African American teachers were and how they were conditioned to socialize African American kids to accept a belief that we were an inferior people. This misleading education process was damaging to me and to every African American who had to endure such a degrading educational system. However, there were a few teachers who understood the damage they could cause if they followed the education process as designed, and they worked hard to uplift kids at Douglass School in Memphis.

When I entered the first grade, I was excited and eager, but in just a few short months, I was labeled a slow learner, placed in a special education class, and held back one year. I recall, as vividly as if it was yesterday, how dejected I was, but as a kid, I had no choice. My mom was unhappy, but like most African Americans during that time, she trusted authority figures, and teachers were near godlike figures, so my mom accepted what she was told regarding my education and inability to learn. I recall pretending to my mom that I was OK with being held back, but my heart was broken, and it never healed from that awful ordeal.

Of course, I now realize that it was not my intellectual ability that held me back, but what Freire and hooks referred to as a "banking system of education." An educational system where students are viewed as obedient users that are required to read, retain, and test. Additionally, the teacher's inability to adequately teach me and many others contributed to the poor education that we received in our early years. If students did not perform in the educational system as designed, they were labeled as "slow" and moved into a class where all the students were told that they were just not smart enough to keep up with the so-called brightest. Yes, we all lived down to the almighty teacher's beliefs, but what's even worse is this: those teachers lived down to the structure of the educational system and became obedient to a system that was designed to destroy the confidence of black boys and force them to behave subserviently.

My mom, Mary Emma, was a proud black woman, and she was inflexible about education for her three children. Her commitment was to see us better educated than her sixth-grade education. As such, she would simply not allow us to skip school, and she did everything that she could with her limited education to assist us with homework and other school activities. I can remember with complete clarity that our mom would not allow us to quit—ever. She would always say, "Dust yourself off and get back in the game, boy."

Growing up, I was very close to my sister, but I was distant from my brother the eldest of the three of us for most of his lifetime. My sister was four years older than me, and she treated me more like her son than a brother, and her love spoiled me. Though she was thin and frail, she would fight anyone to protect me. One of my saddest days was seeing my sister stricken with diabetes. She eventually lost part of one leg to this debilitating disease after surgery in which a doctor left one of his instruments in her stomach, blocking blood flow to her legs.

Due to the incompetence of doctors and indifference to the health of African Americans in Memphis, my sister's condition worsened rapidly. I can't help but wonder, even today, whether she would have fared better if we had the financial resources to have her treated in a hospital located outside of the South. I came to learn, during and after her illness, that African American lives were not as important as the lives of others when it came to health concerns in Memphis and I would learn later that this same mentality was true for most of America. Doctors in Memphis would frequently give up on treating a black person when they would continue their attempt to save the lives of others for the same or similar illnesses. Similar to my mom's faith of being killed in a Memphis hospital by an incompetent nurse, my sister eventually succumbed to her illness because of a doctor's negligence, and no one ever paid for, or apologized for, killing her.

The Sixth-Grade Horror

By the sixth grade, I had regained some confidence in myself, and I believed that I could be whatever I decided to be in America. However, I quickly learned that I was wrong.

While speaking with a guidance counselor, I heard statements that changed my life forever. The counselor asked me what I would like to be when I grew up, and I responded without hesitation, "I would like to be a lawyer." Her response is as clear to me today as when she spoke those words all those years ago: "Oh, no, you could never be a lawyer, Roy, but if you study really hard, you could be a good trash collector, and if you really excel, you could maybe be an electrician." These words changed my perspective of what success might be in America and sent me into a "career" as a gang member at a very early age.

Meeting God

Though I did not understand what had occurred until many years later, one day, while skating, I encountered the presence of God or an angel sent by God for the first time. If I recall correctly, I was about eleven at the time, and I was skating near Douglass High School on Mount Olive Road and Ash Street when my skates became hooked together and I fell to the street. For a moment, I felt as if I had fallen asleep; I suppose I hit my head and blanked out momentarily. Suddenly, a force began to roll me over, while at that same time, a car was speeding down Mount Olive; I could hear the rubber screeching against the hot asphalt. It seemed to take forever, but eventually, the car came to a stop, and the front right wheel rested on my shins and left burn marks that remain today. The driver exited the car and started screaming, "Young man, if you had not rolled out of the street, I would have run over your head!"

At that time, I did not understand what had occurred, but I knew that I did not roll myself out of the street. A very strange external force rolled me over and over until I was safe from death or serious injury. But I was left with a reminder of God's grace forever. For the vast majority of my life, I never told anyone, not even my mother. I have just started to talk about that amazing event recently as I have grown closer to God; I feel it's time for me to share the many miracles that I have witnessed from God.

This is only one of my many encounters with God or his angels over the years; I will write about more in later chapters.

Sports

I loved sports in my early years, and I was actually very good at baseball and football. I played on a summer junior league baseball team and became the starting pitcher. We were very good; in fact, we played well enough to get into the championship round, and I pitched under the lights. What a wonderful memory. I can recall winning the first game and having two base hits. It was here that I developed a thirst for more out of life, but I recalled that a so called educated person had told me that I could never be more than a trash collector, and that thought weighed heavily on my mind, preventing me from being all that God wanted me to be.

I dabbled in football, playing split end for a season, but by now, as a ninth grader, I was working part-time at Kentucky Fried Chicken, and the rigor of practice, school, and work was just too much for me. Once, when I was wrapping up a late-evening practice, the coach called us back on the field and demanded that we give him two more laps. Well, that was enough for me. I promptly went to my locker, showered, and never returned to the football field. I was becoming frustrated with those who were in so-called power positions and those who only wanted to control people…I was growing intellectually, but at the time, I did not understand why or how.

I knew that I was missing something in my life, and I was also feeling as if I could never turn my life around. I felt that America had determined my fate and my future against my own will. I had come to dislike and distrust those who held any position of power—no matter the color of their skin.

Lesson 1: God in Your Life

Black boys, do not allow others to shape your future. You each are a child of the almighty God, and no one can determine your worth but God and you. Be persistent in pursuing your dreams, and learn to love and support one another in your personal lives and in business. As a young boy, I allowed others who were not true mentors or did not really care about my life or future to shape my view of the world, and worse, my negative view of myself—a view that was contradictory to God's view of me. Perhaps I had no other choice at the time, but I am telling you that you can change the perception that you have of yourself, and you can change it now.

The poor, degrading perception of ourselves that we have been, to a great degree, force-fed systematically since our introduction into America has caused us to dislike those we should be embracing, but worst of all, it has caused us to dislike ourselves. Because of the grave mental and physical abuse inflicted upon many of us throughout the years, we have come to see ourselves as lesser and not deserving, but I have great news for you. You came into this world with awesome powers and abilities sewn into the fabric of your being by God Almighty, and no one can take those powers away except you and God.

You have the God-given brainpower to change the world, so start using it today. We all need mentors, and most mean well, but remember that they only have their perspective and perception to reflect onto you; they have no idea or concept of what God has in store for you, as you will see…just read on. Embrace God first, and you will come to see the future that is planned for you, and that future is bright. It is a future that will deliver a life filled with the joy and happiness that you deserve…start with God now.

> But they that wait upon the Lord shall renew their strength;
> they shall mount up with wings as eagles; they shall run,
> and not be weary; and they shall walk, and not faint.
>
> —Isaiah 40:31

> Everyone can rise above their circumstances and achieve success
> if they are dedicated to and passionate about what they do.
>
> —Nelson Mandela

CHAPTER 2

High School

Class

AFTER BEING TOLD THAT I could be no more than a trash collector or an electrician, I lost interest in school, but I was determined to go through the motions of learning because of my mom's great dedication to education. At that time, I could see no benefit to education if I could not pursue my dream career of becoming an attorney. Although I maintained a deep desire to learn, write, and grow intellectually, the stress of being educated in a system that stressed memorizing and reciting information was simply not appealing to me. This yearning for education would never leave me, but again, I did not fully apply myself because the thought of having little or no future to work in the areas that I considered meaningful was disappointing and, frankly, of no interest to me.

I was fortunate enough to excel in a couple classes. Ms. Sanders, my ninth-grade English teacher, had great respect for me, and she spent time ensuring that I did well in class. She allowed me to lead some teamwork assignments, she always called on me in class, she assisted me through my responses, and she was never demeaning to me. I suppose it was because she displayed so much interest in me during class, as did Mr. Garner, my math teacher, that I continued to be interested in education to some degree. I was not an A student in either subject, but I was above average, and my knowledge of both subjects proved to be the reason that I eventually excelled in management and other leadership roles. Yes, these two teachers, whom I will never forget, forced me to maintain my desire to challenge my brain and continue to learn and grow.

I recall my high school years only vaguely because I had become a member of a gang and eventually was the gang leader, and that consumed much of my time. Because of my gang affiliation, most of my teachers were afraid to fail me; they gave me passing grades so that I would not disrupt their class or have one of my gang members damage their car. Obviously, as I reflect on those days, I would definitely change such destructive behavior because my lack of a well-rounded education reared its ugly head in the years to come.

I did graduate from high school, but I was very much unprepared for the world I was about to encounter. My math skills were well above average, and I thought that my writing skills were also, but they were probably at no more than a sixth-grade level, which if I recall correctly was average at Douglass High School. My writing skills were problematic and painfully challenging for me as I pushed for promotions to advanced leadership roles.

Gangbanger

After being told that I could never achieve my dream career, I attempted to diminish my love for education and became a full-fledged gang member with the Down the Hill Boys. Though we never committed any crimes against innocent people and we never stole or robbed, we were considered to be the worst gang in the Midwest by the Memphis Police Department because of our gang fights.

The police often stated, "We will not fly over that neighborhood in a helicopter." The Down the Hill Boys were well known throughout the Memphis area, and becoming the leader was very difficult. I secured the leadership position after a two-hour fight with a very well respected member of our gang by the name of Junebug. He was a tough dude, and if he only knew that I was within seconds of giving up before he raised both hands in defeat, he might have won. The irony of the defeat was that we both were bloody and swollen, so in hindsight, one might say that no one had really won. I became the leader, and that role would prove to be prestigious but very time consuming.

It was during these years that I eventually regained some self-confidence by displaying a tough-guy image and behavior. To be honest, I enjoyed the power and prestige that came with being the gang leader—not to mention the attention I received from girls. It was during my time as a gang leader that I met my lovely wife, Dot, and we are very happily married after forty-four years.

Though I had many dangerous encounters as a gang leader, I was lucky enough to escape without a police record or ever being seriously injured. However, I was scratched with a knife as I stood next to one of my best friends when he was shot in the chest, and he eventually died from that bullet, which rested near his heart.

Another time, when one of my best friends was attacked in a nearby Hollywood neighborhood, I became furious and did something that could have ended badly for many members of my gang. We drove to the party where we believed the rival gang members were. There were several cars of my gang present; I am guessing a dozen members. We were heavily armed, and at that time, we believed that we were prepared to die. We left a half dozen members outside to protect the perimeter, and I entered the party with six members or so, kicking in doors and carelessly pointing our weapons at individuals. We did not find any of the individuals who had attacked my friend, and it was only by the grace of God that we were not engaged by anyone at the party. We left the party and returned to our neighborhood safely. There were many similar occasions, but they are not within the scope of this book.

After I met my lovely wife, I grew tired of the gang life and started to feel the need for something more out of life. I knew that as long as I lived in Douglass, I would have little chance of escaping the grasp of my friends, the alcohol, and untimely trouble with the law, so eventually joined the Air Force and I left Memphis.

Mom

Even today, I would rank my mom as the most intelligent person I ever met, though she only had a sixth-grade education. Basically self-taught, she could read most any book and articulate what she read with great clarity. I was amazed at her ability to read the Bible and to quote many of the passages verbatim. However, what I remember most about my mom was her determination to do more with her life and not to accept the limiting beliefs of others regarding her future.

For many years, my mom worked for Dr. and Mrs. French. They lived in a nice, all-white community by the name of Fraser, and my mom traveled there almost every day to clean their home and raise their children. She was very good at what she did.

Over the years, my mom became very worried about my escalating gang activity, and she was determined to help in any way she could. Concerned about my safety, she confronted me one Friday night, saying that I could not leave the house. In fact, she blocked the front door and barred the back door. She yelled, "You are the worst child that I have, and you will not live to see eighteen." She had heard earlier in the day that my gang was scheduled for a rumble with a rival gang that Friday night. She not only locked me in the house; she refused to let me out of her sight for the weekend. In fact, she insisted that I go to work with her and my stepdad the next day.

Little did I know that this particular Saturday would have the most profound effect on my life up to that point. In fact, my worldview shifted so traumatically that I would never be the same—never, ever. The memories from this visit to my mom's workplace consumed my thoughts for years; in fact, the visuals of that day remain even today with great clarity.

For the most part, my life had consisted of the forty acres that composed Douglass, a community named after the famous Frederick Douglass. Now, for the first time that I could recall in my life, I was headed to the restricted, almost all-white suburbs of Memphis. I saw such beauty that I never knew existed. As my stepdad's friend's car drew closer to the Fraser neighborhood, I noted how clean and well paved the streets were. When we approached the Frenches' home, I noted the four large white stone pillars supporting the front of the four-car-garage home. The yard was immaculate, with lovely pine trees, very tall oak trees, and some that I had no idea what they were except they were shade trees. There were budding flowers everywhere.

I remember that we all went to the backyard, and my mom entered through the back door into the house where she would serve the Frenches breakfast and then take care of the kids for the day. The backyard was even more impressive than the front. There were many trees, but what was most appealing were the kids' gym and other toys, which I was not allowed to touch. My stepdad and I were busy repairing a concrete patio…mixing and pouring concrete for the morning. However, by the afternoon, my life would change forever.

At lunch my mom came to the back door and said, "You all wash up for lunch now." As I reached for the screen door to enter the kitchen area, my stepdad grabbed my shirt and said, "We wash up and eat out here, son." My eyes watered, and my mom's eyes began to water also as she said, "I am sorry, son, but I will have to serve you outside after I have served the Frenches." I never forgot those words: "the Frenches." On that Saturday, my life was forever changed, and even now, my eyes water each time I tell that story, just as they are watering now as I type these lines. From that day forward, I began to ask myself, "Why can't I have this house, this yard, this life?"

I did not realize it at the time, but my mom was affected by that lunchtime experience just as I was. She, too, was changed forever by that experience, and she decided to do something about it. Shortly after that, she began to study and train to become a nurse's aide. It took her six months to complete the training, and I could see the light come on in her eyes as she neared the end. Though she never expressed it verbally, I knew she hated cleaning and caring for Dr. French and his family.

Once she was a nurse's aide, she made more money, had benefits that included insurance and retirement, and worked at a job with professional people. She was setting another example for me with her persistence to improve herself, her life, and our life. I believe that the greatest reward for my mom was being treated with respect and dignity. As awful as that lunchtime experience was, my mom and I both grew in many ways, and most importantly, we found the courage to lift ourselves up and to challenge ourselves to do whatever was necessary to gain some control over our destiny.

My Vision

My life began to take on a different focus after the lunch experience with my mom and after I met Dot, the beautiful young girl who would soon become my wife. After that experience, I found gang life to be less important. I found myself desperately wanting to understand why I was treated with less respect than animals simply because of the color of my skin. I was angry, and I began to thirst for knowledge. For the first time, I was beginning to understand what racism and class difference were, and I was becoming an angry young man. Though I had never hurt a single white person, I could now feel the hate that seemed to be shooting from their eyes in most every encounter. But somehow, in that moment during lunch at the home of the Frenches, I felt a power that I had not experienced previously…I knew that something more was in store for me, but I did not understand what it was or how I would get there.

Though I believed in God and a higher power at that time, I did not believe that I was close to God, and I certainly did not feel that God had a future planned for me, one that I was destined to follow. However, I knew that God placed these words on my lips, and I never forgot them: "Why can't I have this house, this yard, this life?" I also felt a warmth deep down in my stomach, and it was as if God said, "Ask, and you will receive, and I will be with you always." In that moment, fear dissipated, and I felt a courage that gang life never offered. Somehow I knew that my life would improve.

It was shortly after this awful ordeal that I met my soul mate and lovely wife, Dot. We continue to enjoy the love of each other. Because of our strong love, I eventually drifted away from the gang, but I found that I could not completely detach myself because my gang members and other gang members viewed me as the leader of the Down the Hill Boys forever.

I had many scary encounters as a gang member; in fact, they were all scary for me, as a young boy trying to navigate the dangerous streets of my community and Memphis. However, the event that finally convinced me that it was time to leave the gang and the community of Douglass occurred after a Friday-night basketball game. I don't recall whom we played, but I do recall the details of the after-game incident that placed the life of my future wife and my life in danger.

Dot and I left the game early because it was a long walk to her house from the gym. In fact, we had to walk about a half mile or so past my home to get to her home. While we were standing in front of her home, a car pulled up, and a member of a rival gang jumped out of the car with a sawed-off shotgun and pointed it at me. He started to scream that I was responsible for my gang attacking his brother and apparently beating him badly. He was shaking and crying as Dot and I stood there with no way to escape.

This incident occurred after the experience at the home of the Frenches. I was sixteen or seventeen—I don't recall which—but I was not afraid, and I wanted to protect Dot. I put my hands out and started to shout, "Shoot me—I have lived my life, and I am not afraid to die." I continued until he finally jumped back in his vehicle with his gang members and left. As I reflect on those days, I now realize that I was protected by a higher power…by God. Later Dot's mom told us that she was watching at the door and had prepared a shotgun to use at any moment. Let's be clear here: while I was not afraid in that moment because I knew I had the presence of God, I was generally scared to death as a gang member, just as most gang members were. Let it be known that those who participate in gangs today are afraid as well.

Lesson 2: Family, Friends, and Your Life
These lessons taught me much; I learned a major lesson: that gang life is destructive both mentally and physically to the individual who is leading such a life and to those whom the individual should be embracing and supporting. The years I dedicated to the life of being a gang member were wasted in virtually every way, and those years would have served me best if I had been studying and growing intellectually. I should have been about building my brothers up, not tearing them down. I should have embraced my brothers and shared love and support toward them. All of the gang members should have found ways to help one another to be better members of our society, and we should have found ways to make our community better, both financially and intellectually, for ourselves and for those who would follow us.

Though I had my mother's unconditional love and support, I was unhappy because of the negative environment I had to engage in every day of my childhood. I was unhappy because I had been told by authorities at school that I had very limited opportunities in my future. There were no African American heroes at that time in my community to look up to, and no positive role models to follow. As such, I gravitated to a life involving gang activity. Today, you have many successful heroes to look up to and follow. Please don't miss the opportunity to tap into their expertise and to lift one another up, even if you only have the capacity to read about them.

You have a burning passion to be something special in our conflicted society...an attorney, doctor, scientist, professor, CEO, legislator, and so on. Take some time and identify that passion, then find someone that you can share your passion with, someone who can help you grow. Believe me, that someone, a passionate mentor, is waiting to embrace you.

You are wonderfully built, unique, one of a kind. Ever wonder why no one else in the whole world has the same fingerprints as you? It's because you are special, and you were made to leave positive prints on this wonderful earth.

Just as I did as a young man, many of you have bought into the negative images that others have bestowed upon you. You believe these negative images so deeply that you feel that it is OK to treat one another with disrespect and to hurt others. Well, it's not OK. Let's start today to build one another up—start to use the beautiful brains that God blessed you with. Find that passion within that can change the world. Spend time with the Bible, and God will help you to identify that passion within you. Seek support from family and friends, and start to live your passion, your dream.

If you do nothing else, simply love and support one another starting today, right now. Treat everyone as if they are a family member or friend, not a foe, and watch your life begin to change instantly. You have enough other people disrespecting your life. Don't join hand in hand with them...love yourself, your family, your friends, your neighbors. Finally, stop hurting one another. You have a very powerful future ahead, which you will learn about in chapter 10, but you must start to prepare for that future now. You cannot wait.

> Darkness cannot drive out darkness; only light can do that.
> Hate cannot drive out hate; only love can do that.
>
> —MARTIN LUTHER KING JR.

CHAPTER 3

The Air Force

Mentors, Friends, and a Test

In 1970 my brother was fighting the war in Vietnam as a military policeman, a war that he did not understand but a war that he fought because he was drafted and because his country required him to do so, just as many African American males have done in years past. Yes, he was a military police officer, responsible for protecting the soldiers while they rested and recuperated after hours and sometimes days in the field, fighting enemies America had termed the Viet Cong. Though my brother and I were not very close, he did demonstrate his love for me by asking me not to join the army when my lottery number was selected. He was very explicit in his desire for me to join the navy or air force before I was drafted, and he had personal reasons—many of which he could not discuss because of the pain from his time in the war zone, but he did share one.

He told me about a young Vietnamese kid, maybe eleven or twelve years of age. This kid came through their camp each day and tossed a ball to my brother; they would play catch for a while. However, one day when the kid came to camp, things were different. The kid was not bouncing his usual ball, and as he prepared to toss it to my brother, one of my brother's peers screamed, "It's a bomb!" and my brother, along with other soldiers, shot and killed the kid. They did confirm that he was carrying a bomb with the potential to kill and wound many soldiers; my brother was never the same. I am sure that for this reason and many others, he did not wish for me to be involved in the actual war. Thus, I attempted to join the air force.

I considered the Navy, but I was not a very good swimmer, and deep water scared me, so I decided to take the air force entry exam. To my surprise, and the surprise of the air force examining officers, my results were outstanding. For the first time in my life, I was considered intelligent, and this was our government confirming my intellect. I was a bit confused because I was told for many years by those I now know to be uninformed teachers that my future was limited because of my lack of intelligence. Only one individual ever articulated this explicitly, but many teachers made it very clear implicitly that we African Americans were limited intellectually. As a young kid, I was affected by such claims, and they continued to have a profound negative influence on my psyche. Now, after a full day with a team of air force examiners, I was as shocked as they were to learn that I really had a pretty good brain—to discovered that I was, in fact, intelligent.

I was all set to enter the air force, but suddenly they put everything on hold pending an investigation as to whether I cheated on the exam. I was, once again, devastated and confused by these events. Their investigation included reviewing video, interviewing those who tested with me, and going through my community speaking with neighbors and teachers. After weeks of investigating, they finally concluded that I did not cheat on the exam; thus, I could enter the air force.

Because I had been systematically taught for so long that I was not intelligent, I was again shocked and scared when an air force recruiter offered me the choice of three different jobs. One sergeant later told me that this was very unusual, but because of my high test score, several departments in the air force had requested me for their team.

I was offered the choice of dental tech/hygienist, air traffic controller, or secret police. However, I believed that my decision-making skills were very limited at that time, and because I had been socialized to see myself as not intelligent, I was afraid to select the job I really wanted, which was the air traffic controller position. I simply did not believe that I had the cognitive capacity to be either secret police or air traffic controller. As such, I selected my position in the air force based on the one that I feared the least: the dental tech/hygienist job.

One reason I was afraid of the air traffic controller position was that I had never been on an airplane, and the thought of flying scared me. Though I was fairly good at math and science, I feared the thought of helping pilots land planes. I worried that one mistake could cause a tragic accident and cost lives. Even though I had often carried a gun as a gang leader, I was always afraid… as such, I could not see myself with a gun or in dangerous situations as secret police. Thus, I selected the dental tech/hygienist position—a mistake.

Training

For nine months I was at Sheppard Air Force Base in Texas, in class from 7:00 a.m. to 7:00 p.m., seven days a week, not including study time, learning to be a medic. This training was the most intellectually challenging experience of my life, with the possible exception of my Ph.D. studies. I learned health-care knowledge that improved my life and the lives of many in my family and others. In fact, the lifesaving skills I was taught during this extensive and exhausting training prepared me to save the life of a baby that was drowning in a bathtub in a nearby apartment when we lived in Denver, Colorado.

After medic training, I started dental technician training, which is the same as a dental hygienist in the civilian world. I recall that the dental hygienist training was much easier and more fun than training to be a medic. This education served to benefit my family more than I could ever have imagined. I became a dental hygiene instructor, and I educated my family using the same hygiene lessons as I taught the soldiers. Because of the excellent training, my family generally had excellent hygiene; we knew the importance of flossing and brushing at least twice a day, and more if required. We also learned the best brushing techniques, and we were introduced to toothbrushes that promoted excellent dental hygiene.

Now for the first time in my life, I met individuals with varying backgrounds, different skin colors, different dialects, and different personal and religious beliefs, but we all had one thing in common: we were protecting our country, America in the Air Force. As such, we were a real team and friends to the end. I had many great experiences in the air force—so many, in fact, that I could write a book all its own. Because of my wonderful air force experience, I feel compelled to share a few exciting stories with you.

My First Plane Flight

We flew Braniff Airways from Memphis to an airport near Lackland Air Force Base in San Antonio, Texas. I recall that the first half of the flight was generally smooth, but I was nervous. As we approached the base, the plane began to shake violently, and I became extremely concerned; however, the worst was yet to come. Someone on the plane yelled out, "Why are we circling the airport?" We had circled several times. The pilot finally came over the airway and said, with a very choppy and less-than-confident voice, "We have lost one engine, and we are circling to burn off fuel in case of a crash landing." Suddenly you could hear people crying and sighing with fear. Yes, that included me.

After circling for what seemed forever, the plane started its descent toward the runway. The pilot came over the intercom again and said much more calmly, "We are going to attempt a landing. Please place yourself in a crash landing position. The flight attendant will assist you."

As I peered out the window, I could see emergency vehicles lined up around the runway for what seemed miles and miles. This was by far the scariest day of my life. Of course, I began to reflect on and apologize for some of the terrible deeds I had committed. I thought about the people I would miss and how I could and would change if I were spared. This was another event that proved to me that there is a God. It was also clear that I had a higher purpose and that I would be spared even if there was a crash.

The plane continued its very wobbly descent due to the lost engine and eventually made a perfect landing on the runway to loud screams of joy. In fact, I am not sure I have ever been on a plane that made such a landing, one that was perfectly smooth. All the new recruits, pilots, and flight attendants were now yelling and screaming with joy, as were the men and women who were surrounding the emergency vehicles. Yes, with each similar event, my faith in God grew stronger, and my understanding of my purpose started to unfold.

My Best Friend

I met Freddie while in my first assignment at Lowry Air Force Base dental clinic in Denver. Freddie was the first Mexican American I had ever met, and it was the most wonderful friendship I had experienced. For the first time, I knew someone who was not interested in being macho or proving that he was better, stronger, or smarter. Freddie just wanted to be my friend and for me to be his friend in return. We talked and laughed every chance we had. We were both initially placed on the dental specialist floor as dental technicians. Freddie was placed with the chair of the dental department, a major and endodontist, and I was placed with Colonel English, a prosthodontist. I often wondered why a major was the chair of the dental specialist team when a ranking colonel was in the same department, but I never asked.

Freddie and his wife, Rosa, introduced Dot and me to Mexican food. They prepared homemade tacos, and I loved every bite. Dot was reluctant and did not eat very much at that time, but later in life she became a greater lover of Mexican food than I. Freddie and I never had the chance to do many guy things because he seemed to be sick much of the time. After a very short visit at the base clinic, Freddie was diagnosed with a form of cancer in his shoulder, and eventually his arm was removed. Shortly after the surgery, he passed away. His wife, Rosa, relocated back to Mexico to be with her family. I miss Freddie even today because his was the first friendship that was unconditional. For the first time in my life, I had a friend who needed no proof of worth. He was simply my friend.

My First Mentor

Dr. English was my first mentor in the air force, and he was the smartest and nicest man I had met. When I entered the air force, I had two gold teeth in the front of my mouth, and Dr. English said, "Roy, you know those two teeth have to go." My first American social lesson from Dr. English was understanding that I would not be given the opportunity to achieve my dreams here in America with gold teeth in the front of my mouth. He said, "Roy, you will not be allowed at the table of success with gold teeth displayed when you smile that warm smile."

Each time we had a patient cancel or a no-show, Dr. English would start to work on my teeth. In addition to two gold teeth, I had several cavities because we were not taught the proper way to care for our teeth in the hood. In fact, I learned about dental floss for the first time in the air force. Back home in Memphis, we only saw a dentist when we were in pain, and the dentist in Memphis had one remedy for African Americans: extraction.

In a very short time, I became the lead technician in the specialty department, and soon I was promoted to a corporal. Although I did not realize it at the time, I was much more intelligent than I had been led to believe back home in Memphis; in fact, I proved to be the best noncommissioned officer employee in the clinic other than Master Sergeant George W. Thomas, the first African American man I ever met who carried himself as a proud black man. I swear he feared no one.

A short time after my first promotion, I was again promoted—this time to a sergeant and noncommissioned officer in charge (NCOIC) of the base dental services. Though I had led the largest gang in the Mid-South, I did not understand the leadership skills needed; I did not realize that those same skills that had served me well as the leader of a gang could serve me well in a professional environment with doctors and dentists; however, Master Sergeant George W. Thomas knew.

I had been so brainwashed by the negative social environment in Memphis that my self-confidence and self-awareness were nonexistent. Back in Memphis, I was basically relegated to a social system that had systematically convinced most blacks, including me, that we were to be subservient and that our lives were to be used to serve and to destroy one another, and we followed that craziness blindly. Even as it destroyed our family, friends, and community, we continued that unnatural behavior—behavior that our ancestors had endured during slavery but never practiced within their tribes back in the homeland.

In the air force, I struggled to embrace my true self; I had been socialized to be what others perceived my human worth to be. I had been taught that the only place I had the authority to prove my true worth was in black communities among black boys like me, and no one cared if we hurt one another in order to prove our self-worth. As such, we perpetrated the same cruelty on one another that had been heaped on us and our ancestors during slavery and the Jim Crow period. This was a classic example of "social learning theory." Yes, we had been trained to control situations with brutality, and sadly, we carried out and continue to carry out acts against other African Americans today. It is time that we understand that the past does not equal the future and that our past training here in America is not congruent with most African cultures. It's a learned behavior that was forced upon us during slavery, and it is one that we can unlearn.

I Am Intelligent

Master Sergeant George W. Thomas became my greatest mentor and supporter, as you will see shortly…read on.

A short man at about five feet five inches tall but with a big, bold presence, he was African American, and other than my mother, the smartest person I ever met. Like my mother, Master Sergeant Thomas only had a high school education, but his grasp of the English language was better than any teacher I ever met at Douglass High School in my thirteen years there. For the first time, I met a black man who was not afraid to address any white man as an equal. Sergeant Thomas did not shrink away in any situation, and he never appeared to be afraid. His demeanor demanded dignity, respect, and personal honor. In fact, if he did not have stripes on his shoulders, you would have sworn that he was the general in charge of Lowry Air Force Base.

Sergeant Thomas saw something in me that I had been too blind to see for my entire eighteen years of life. He saw the intelligence in me that I worked extremely hard to suppress because I had been told that my cognitive capacity was limited and that I was not smart because of the color of my skin, which upon reflection is, of course, a socialization process intended to keep African Americans as common laborers.

As I reflect now on the early years of my life, I realize that the black teachers had been systematically socialized through our biased education system to see other blacks as lacking the capacity to achieve very much in life. They had been socialized and trained to see us as unintelligent, and they had been convinced that our upward mobility or future success was limited to service-level jobs. I also understand now that they felt some sense of superiority because some had obtained a college education, but many were only high school graduates with a teaching certificate. Shameful as it was, I understand that the systematic degrading of blacks had become embedded at a very deep cognitive level in many of our teachers even during their educational process; as such, they believed with all their hearts that they were doing what was best for the black youth of our society. They believed faithfully that our intellect was limited and that the American social system required that they restrict our career opportunities to a few labor intensive and thankless jobs. If only they had studied the history of Africa and African American history—our real history.

Today I also understand that my friends and other youth that I grew up with were just as convinced as I that they were limited cognitively and had a very limited future. Thus, they, like our teachers, would work very hard to reinforce the belief that our future growth was limited and that to transcend the race barrier was virtually impossible. In fact, those of us who attempted to grow outside the community found ourselves at war with words that served to confirm and ensure that each of us remembered our place in society and that each of us fought to keep us all together at the bottom of the barrel. Yes, we had been trained well. I remember vividly that we would make statements such as "You think you are white," "Don't be an Uncle Tom," and "Remember your place."

In fact, when I was young, my favorite TV star was Roy Rogers; I would occasionally dress like a cowboy, and the demeaning words would start. Many of the boys in the community would yell, "Look at the cowboy!" so I eventually stopped being a cowboy. Now understand that, even if those words were spoken in jest, they rendered long-term mental damage to me and many black boys who lived in similar situations. These words caused mental damage that we struggle to overcome throughout much of our lives.

NCO of the Year Contest

I was on vacation, relaxing with my family, when I received an urgent call from Master Sergeant Thomas's assistant. I answered the phone and promptly stated that I was on vacation. She responded, "But the master sergeant needs to see you right away." She refused to explain any further, and I knew that I had no choice but to meet Sergeant Thomas on the base at the dental clinic. I was stationed at Lowry Air Force Base in Denver, Colorado, and the base was in walking distance of our apartment; as such, I had no excuse, so I went to meet Sergeant Thomas.

After approximately eight hours with Sergeant Thomas, my life would never be the same again…ever. Sergeant Thomas first said that he had a great opportunity for the dental clinic, the air force base, and me. He then told me that he wanted me to compete in a contest in which I could be named the noncommissioned officer of the year (NCOIC)—not just for our base, but for the entire air force. He also explained how that title would be a prestigious example for the base and for me. He further explained that all I had to do was answer questions about several different subjects. I don't recall all the subjects, but I do remember that they included military and American history, math, and some personal questions. My first response was, "I can't do that." My second response was, "I am not smart enough." And my third response was, "With all due respect, Master Sergeant, I will not do that." That last response was the wrong response.

For the first time in almost eighteen months on base, I experienced both the anger and love of Master Sergeant Thomas simultaneously. His face became swollen, veins popped up in his neck, he started to perspire, and he proceeded to yell at the top of his voice. For the next eight hours or so, with the exception of a short meal break, at which time I could not eat, he screamed at me—shouting only positive statements. He yelled statements like, "You are the smartest airman on this damned base"—I doubt that even today, because if I recall, at its peak, there were some forty thousand airmen on base. He continued to yell all day, telling me to believe in myself, have faith in myself, and trust in my intelligence and all my abilities. At one point, he showed extreme disappointment in me, and then he grabbed me around the chest, tossed me against the wall, and gave me a big hug, saying, "You are smart, Roy. Please believe what I tell you, and please believe in yourself."

I, of course, had no option but to accept his request, or demand, if you will, to participate in this important contest for our base. Of course, my vacation was over. The preparation for the contest lasted for several weeks, which included quizzes and help from professional soldiers and air force educators. The week finally arrived for the competition to start. I learned that I was competing against all military branches, and that, to me, was even more frightening. After the three- or four-day contest ended, I was named the third best of all the competitors, and there were more than a dozen participating finalists, if I recall correctly. Yes, Master Sergeant Thomas had confirmed for me that I was a bright young man and that I should be proud of my intelligence. After the contest, I was invited to teach dental hygiene on the base and in the community, and I was placed on several committees, including the diversity committee. Master Sergeant Thomas treated me as his son until I left the air force in 1974.

Diversity Training

As I think back to my time in the air force, I realize that the air force was far ahead of the rest of the country regarding embracing diversity in many respects. For example, growing up in Memphis, I could never envision having white friends, but most of my friends during my air force days were white or Latino, and that continues today. This proved to be a wonderful educational opportunity for me in terms of learning to trust those who are different. However, my greatest educational experience might have been becoming acutely aware of the fact that I could not only compete in an environment that was mostly white, but I could win—even though my previous educational experience at Douglass was generally poor at best, with a few exceptions. I realized that if I could compete in an environment like the air force, which only accepted the brightest of our society at that time, I could lead in almost any challenging situation, regardless of who was involved.

Our diversity training and diversity meetings were very warm and friendly, unlike the diversity training sessions I experienced in the corporate world (more on that later). Our meetings brought soldiers together, and we talked about our similarities, not our differences. We discussed how we were one people and one team. However, as much as I had grown, I continued to doubt my intellect and my abilities to compete.

I recall one diversity meeting where we were all challenged to write a poem, and I was very reluctant. This was 1972, and I have never shared that poem with the general public until this book. As you read the poem, please understand that a young man at about the age of nineteen wrote this in 1972, and he was still struggling with understanding the negative social system that he grew up in and the new social system he was embracing in the air force, which was generally positive and embracing. Though I had grown intellectually, I was stuck in a time warp of the past, and this poem helped me to move on with my life. I recall reading this poem in one diversity training meeting in the air force and receiving applause from all who were present. My view today is far from being radical. In fact, my wife has occasionally accused me of being a strict conservative, though that is not the case. I think that we would all be kidding ourselves if we believed that none of this was true, even today, as I write this portion of my book.

The poem…

Life for Me

Life is a struggle for people like me, for people with Black skin just like me.
We have been murdered, raped, and stripped of our rights…those people that did this, you know, are White.
The Black has pulled through slavery and oppression, but we still must fight for any satisfaction.
They say that we are free and have all rights; if this is true, then why must we fight?
The White man is nothing but a boy; he's treated the Black man as an automatic toy.

Now the Black man is advancing very fast, and the boy is afraid that he'll soon live the past.

Leaving the Air Force

As I prepared to leave the air force after four years of successful service, I was somewhat conflicted because I had found a support structure filled with love that I had not felt in Memphis, with the exception of my mother. I was afraid to leave the safe zone of the air force, but there was such a strong internal desire to go back home that I could not overcome it; thus, we would return to Memphis. I recall later viewing this as one of the biggest mistakes of my life.

I recall telling Master Sergeant Thomas that I had decided to leave the air force to return to Memphis, my hometown. I expected Sergeant Thomas to be angry, for after all, he had worked extremely hard to shape me into a leader modeled after himself. Sergeant Thomas had lost his son in an unfortunate auto accident just after I had arrived on base, and I had become his son's replacement…he really did love me as a son. When I told him that I was leaving, I was surprised that he was supportive because he wanted me to be happy. What I did not expect was his boss's response.

Colonel Daugherty was extremely upset that I was leaving as the NCOIC of the dental administrative services at Lowry Air Force Base. Though I had been recognized and promoted several times, I did not realize how good I was until I announced that I was leaving the air force. Yes, I was still suffering from the extreme negative socialization process of my childhood, and I was still struggling with my identity: I found it mentally difficult to see myself as smart and deserving of the leadership role that I had earned.

A bald man with a very distinguished appearance, Colonel Daugherty was generally a nice person. In fact, he started the conversation by asking me to stay on and to continue to serve our country. However, when I explained, in a matter-of-fact tone, that I was leaving the air force, his voice and personality began to change. He first stated that I signed an agreement to stay in the air force for an additional two years because of the education I received, but he admitted that the document was misplaced and could not be located; as such, he did not have the authority to force me to stay in the air force. I continued to repeat that I was leaving, and he became extremely angry. I saw a side of Colonel Daugherty that I had not witnessed previously…he started to yell, and here is the one thing he said that was extremely hurtful. He uttered, "Your kids will get sick, and you will not have the means to care for them if you get out of the air force, Sergeant Whitmore." Colonel Daugherty left the office, and Master Sergeant Thomas entered.

Master Sergeant Thomas hugged me and said, "Let's keep in touch, Mr. Whitmore." He also apologized for the colonel's behavior, and he congratulated me, stating that during the time I led the dental administrative services, the clinic did not have a single complaint, and that was the reason Colonel Daugherty was fighting with such vigor to keep me on board. It's amazing that I did not understand my worth at that time.

Sears Takes Me to Red Lobster

After leaving the air force, I was lucky enough to land a very good job with Sears in the Raleigh Spring Mall in Memphis. I was hired on the first interview with the store manager and department managers. Several department managers wanted me on their team, but Don Hampton, the manager in sewing machines and vacuums, fought hardest to get me on his team. In a few short months, Don and I had developed a very strong mentor-mentee relationship. Within the first year, I had become the number-one salesman in the department. Once I had the number-one salesman title, Sears offered me all types of perks, such as dinner out and free steaks. I worked in a city sales event where the top salesperson was the only one writing tickets and had a personal cashier—those sales days were big paydays!

One quarter, I became the top salesperson in Memphis, and my manager and other regional leaders in Memphis wanted to take me to dinner. I refused because I was uncomfortable eating in places that hosted predominately white clientele. I continued to refuse, and finally Don Hampton, my manager, asked me to do him a big favor and just stop by Red Lobster to have one cocktail with him and the regional team. He said that he would be honored because I was his top salesperson and he owed me at least one congratulation toast. He was a very good boss, and I had great respect for Don, so I reluctantly agreed to join him for one cocktail. However, when I arrived, the entire leadership team was present, and they had a reservation for all of us.

I recall being very nervous and uncomfortable as I took my seat because I was the only African American in the restaurant. As I sat down, I tried to remember proper etiquette from my air force days, and I tried to find something on the menu that was appealing. Don noticed that I was uncomfortable, and he asked if he could order something that he loved and thought I would like. He ordered crab-stuffed shrimp and rib-eye steak. I had never had crab-stuffed shrimp, and was it ever delicious!

Don and the other leaders made me feel like I was a part of the team. Don said, "Etiquette be damned. We are here to celebrate you, Roy. Enjoy!" I am thankful to Don for being a mentor and a friend. Even down in Memphis, he did not allow skin color to determine his friends or whom he would dine with.

Finally, I was coming out of my shell a bit. My confidence was growing because I had a mentor who cared about me. I was beginning to embrace my intelligence and start thinking about more education. In fact, I fell in love with Red Lobster, and my family and I dined there several times each month. Even today, I occasionally crave Red Lobster's food.

Lesson 3: Mentors and Your Life

I believe that it was Earl Nightingale in his famous book *Lead the Field* who stated, "You can have anything in this life that you want if you just help enough other people get what they want." I read that many years ago, and I never forgot that statement because it is true. It's not just about working hard. It's also about education, mentors, trusting in God, and helping others. When your parents told you to work hard and said that you had to be better than your peers, what they really should have been saying was to get more education. With more education you can compete and win with your peers. Don't get me wrong—working hard is important, but education will help you to work smarter and advance farther.

My mentors in the air force—Master Sergeant George W. Thomas and Dr. English—taught me that supporting my team members was much more powerful than finding a reason to compete with them. Remember that we have been systematically taught to compete with one another, to strive to be better than one another, and we continue to live that craziness even today. Please read and study the real African American history and our systematic mental conditioning during slavery, the Jim Crow laws, and other cognitive development processes that conditioned us to feel, behave, and be seen as inferior—particularly if one does not win in every encounter and in every situation.

It's funny that by altering the cognitive development of African Americans to be subservient, the white males who perpetrated heinous acts upon African Americans were actually convincing themselves that they were superior to African Americans, women, and others whom they perceived to be different or less. This unshakable conviction can be seen in the behavior of too many white males today and is proof that no one wins when one attempts to force his or her beliefs on another.

Become a mentor, find a mentor, and start supporting one another today in every endeavor. Display only love and support for one another…become a unit of intellectual growth. Most of all, when great success is bestowed upon you, share the knowledge and wisdom that you have attained with your brothers. Only through love, support, and education can we change the direction of our brothers and be recognized for our great gifts to America and the world. One day in the not so distant future, you will be the most powerful voting bloc in America. I'll tell you how, why, and when later.

> One of the things I keep learning is that the secret of
> being happy is doing things for other people.
>
> —Dick Gregory

CHAPTER 4

Target Stores

IT WAS SPRING OF 1983, and I was an assistant store manager with JB Hunter Discount Stores, soon to become Jefferson Ward Discount Stores, in Memphis, just down the street from Elvis Presley's home. Jefferson Ward was a subsidiary of Montgomery Ward and a very progressive discount store chain primarily located in Florida. We were in the middle of completing a summer transition…one that should have taken five days to complete, but I led a team that completed the transition in three days. On the third day, toward the end of the set being completed, three guys walked up to me and introduced themselves as executives from Target stores, a retail organization that I had not heard of previously. One human resource executive, Ormond Curl, asked if he could speak with me in private, and I agreed. He said that they were at our store the previous two days watching as I led a team that worked the summer transition set and that Target would like to offer me a job. Ormond said, "We would pay you twice what you are making if you can start in a week." I asked, "Would you like to know what I am making?" and Ormond, who is now my business partner and friend, replied, "No, just bring a copy of your last check stub when you report, and I will double your pay." Of course I accepted, and my Target experience started…one that would prove to be problematic in the end.

After completing my training in Memphis and leaving Target for a short period for reasons I do not recall, I returned. Shortly after my return, I was relocated to Denver. There I became a store manager in training and quickly moved into the largest-volume store in Denver (T-6) as an assistant store manager. Approximately eighteen months later, I became the store manager at Target T-40 in the Denver area. This is the store where my team and I would change Target forever.

Store Manager: The N Word

As a store manager, I had the opportunity to become a member of the elite group for Target in Denver. I could hang out with the district manager and the regional staff after work to share ideas and talk about our business and, of course, personal life, as well. I had become a member of the group that would ultimately lead and change Target someday.

In fact, at one point I was labeled as high potential and was invited to go on a weeklong retreat at the University of Miami with many other high-potential managers from around the country to study "political science." They wanted us to learn how to be politically correct if we were to represent Target as executives someday. There were twenty-four high-potential managers at the training event, and all were eventually promoted to director-level positions or higher.

I really felt a part of the Denver team, and I was having fun learning and growing. However, one night while we were out having dinner and drinks, one of the staff members said, "And I told that nigger..." I don't recall the end of the statement, but I sure remember the N-word. I had blended into the all-white team so well that they forgot that I was an African-American. There was a moment of complete silence as I stood up and walked away. Shortly after that N-word was spoken, each of the managers came up to me and apologized individually, and they also apologized as a group. They were sincere, and they had no idea what caused one member to behave in such a way and to utter such a statement. This was another event that motivated me to learn more about human behavior. How could individuals I had found not to be racist or biased slip into a cognitive state that would cause them to behave in such a way and utter such a racist word? Our relationship remained stable, but my trust in the team had diminished.

The War Strategy vs. Walmart

In spring 1985, a Walmart sign went up just down the hill from my store, and when Walmart was coming, it was generally time to be afraid. However, for some reason I was not afraid, and not to be overly religious, but again, I believe that God or angels were by my side at that time as well. Maybe it was because I had already enjoyed some early success at Target in terms of helping to create several new programs, which included overnight stocking and a backroom initiative that would make it very easy for employees to locate product when needed for stocking the floor or serving the customer. We started planning our Walmart "war strategy"—a strategy that would break many Target rules and some long-held policies.

My team and I developed a plan that included training all employees to operate a register so that we would never have lines of more than two customers at any register while a customer was being served. In fact, we created what we termed as a one-plus-one checkout rule: never more than one customer being checked out and one waiting. We knew that Walmart would have lines, and we knew that customers in our area valued their time, so speed at the checkout was a strategic advantage for us. This one-plus-one standard is now followed by many retailers throughout America. We also cross-trained employees into several positions, so that we always had coverage for every department.

Next, prior to Walmart's opening, we went down near their sign and conducted pep rallies. It was a blast. Additionally, each department led a rally every Monday morning before the store opened, boasting about how we would beat up on Walmart. The final part of our plan was the price challenge: we decided that we would not allow Walmart to beat us on price. We matched Walmart prices, including their sale prices, and this was a big no-no at Target.

In fact, Target executives had resigned themselves to losing 30 percent of store sales, 25 percent of store profits, and 20 percent of their best employees to Walmart each time Walmart opened a store within a mile or so of a Target store. This had become an accepted fact, and they fervently believed they could not affect the planned losses to Walmart. They had accepted defeat. I was puzzled that such smart people at Target could ever plan to give away business without any fight at all. In fact, one VP learned about our war strategy, and he threatened to fire me if I went forward with the plans. Ironically, my district manager turned a blind eye to what we were doing and never said a word.

Well, we changed those numbers, and as Ken Macke, the CEO, exclaimed in an executive meeting, "If not for Roy, we would be out of business in five years." Figure 1 is a copy of the note he left our team after coming to visit us during the holiday season to thank us for teaching Target how to compete with Walmart. Our war strategy saved Target millions, and possibly billions, of dollars over the years.

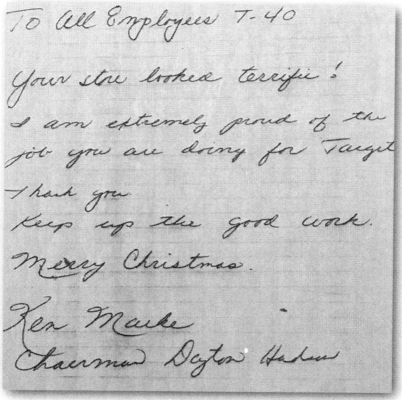

Figure 1. A note from Ken Macke, Target Chairmen and Chief Executive Officer to our team.

The results from our store were amazing. We only lost one employee to Walmart, and that was not a critical position. However, what was most amazing was that we lost virtually no sales and only 10 percent of our profit as compared to the previous year. The results were so phenomenal that virtually every Target executive came to visit our store to learn more about what we had done, and of course, the executive who threatened to fire me, an African American, was now a big supporter. The CEO, Ken Macke, and president, Bob Ulrich, bought me lunch and grilled me about what we did because they were excited to share it with the board and the entire organization.

During that time, my college education had been limited to a few classes at Metro State College in Denver, and I found it difficult to explain exactly what we did to achieve such great success versus Walmart, and of course, all of the personal attention made me very uncomfortable.

Shortly after the results were announced to the company, I received a call from a reporter at *Fortune* magazine. The reporter had been authorized by Target's media department to speak with me, but I was so nervous that I could not really express myself or articulate what we actually did to diminish the Walmart effect on our store. Thus, the article was never published. I missed this exciting opportunity because I was not prepared. I had not prepared myself for such success. Although I had been labeled as very intelligent in the air force, the lack of formal education was starting to affect my performance. An opportunity that might have pushed me in a different direction in life, had I applied myself in high school and completed my undergraduate degree, slipped through my fingers. Although I had grown intellectually in the air force, I did not have the formal education that could have helped me develop my critical thinking abilities; as such, I simply could not take advantage of this great opportunity—an opportunity that might have opened doors that were far beyond my imagination.

Shortly after the Walmart war strategy had proved to be extremely successful, Ken Macke and Bob Ulrich insisted that I move to Minneapolis and manage our test store…T-240 in Brooklyn Park, Minnesota. Although Ken Macke and Bob Ulrich declared me the savior of Target, I never shared in Target's vast wealth as many underachievers did, and even those who made little or no significant difference in the success of Target were given greater raises, bonuses, and stock options. Again I wondered, why? How is that possible?

This is one reason why, when I started my PhD program at Fielding Graduate University, I wanted to understand the dynamics that were at play in the C-suite; I wanted to understand why people of color and women were not allowed to share in the vast wealth of Fortune 1000, 500, and 100 organizations. This quest to understand how one can make such a big difference in an organization and never really be recognized for that contribution was a burning desire for me. This burning desire drove me to obtain four degrees, including a PhD in human development from an academically well-respected university. I really wanted to understand this crazy phenomenon.

The Spotlight and Regional Staff

During the year that I held the store manager position at T-240 in Brooklyn Park, Minnesota, we developed new innovative approaches for business at Target. My store championed the snack bar with Pizza Hut that Target continues to operate today. The backroom stocking procedures and overnight stocking procedures were refined to improve product flow and, ultimately, productivity. Team training and a "fast, fun, and friendly" approach to customer service, which was a product of my store, was implemented in all stores. The shelf labels were revised, adding the actual space numbers, so stockers could quickly determine what item was missing and if an item was out of place or needed to be stocked. This new label also helped the staff and management teams to easily identify when an item was missing, thus improving shelf stock and sales in all Target stores coast to coast.

I also argued for a baby-changing table to be added in the men's room. It was finally added, and many store managers and customers began to ask for it in other Target stores in the city. Eventually, changing tables were added to the men's room in every store and became an accepted standard in men's rooms in all industries throughout America.

It was also in this store that an unnamed mentor emerged. To this day, I have no idea who he or she was. This mentor was very smart and clearly powerful as well; he or she was aware of my every move, it seemed. He or she would send me notes weekly telling me how to improve. For example, if I sent out a memo with grammatical issues, I would receive a memo explaining what was wrong and how to correct it. This individual also suggested educational tapes for grammar and speaking, and I took full advantage of those suggestions. Because I did not apply myself in high school, I felt inadequate when writing during that period in my life. I would oftentimes think, "If I had only applied myself in high school…" During those days, constructing a coherent sentence in writing was very painful for me; as such, I communicated verbally as often as possible.

When challenged to write a memo, I occasionally placed my head in my hands and almost came to tears. I wished that I had applied myself in school instead of engaging in gang activities. I wished I had listened to my mother and those few teachers who really cared about me. And, yes, I prayed for help. I also started to wonder if I could ever do that which I so desperately wanted to do—obtain an undergraduate degree. I just did not think it was possible, and I was busy trying to succeed at Target, so time for school appeared to be limited. Today, I realize that succeeding would have been much easier if I had only applied myself in high school and gone on to complete college.

After one year in the test store, I was promoted to the regional staff, where I was responsible for parts of Target stores that we called hardlines. These sections included sporting goods, hardware, and a few other areas. It was in this role that I came face-to-face with internal operations of Target and came to better understand how management selections were made. Most importantly, I was in a position that allowed me the opportunity to compare my abilities and intellect with those who were considered the brightest and most talented leaders at Target. It was in this position that I recognized my amazing memory. In fact, my memory was a magnet for details and facts.

However, my deficient writing abilities continued to be an area of focus for those who wanted to derail my career, and there were many. I recall the regional senior vice president saying after reading one of my memos, "I know what you meant, Roy." This left me feeling dejected; though I do not believe that he intended to make me feel uncomfortable, nevertheless, I did feel very ill prepared because of my poor writing skills. The good news was that I was a very good reader, and my memory and reading skills would be the catalysts to propel me to the next two levels in my career at Target.

I had many big wins as a regional staff member because of my excellent memory. In fact, I memorized all the policies and procedures from three binders that averaged, I suppose, some two hundred pages each. During regional meetings when someone challenged a policy or procedure, the senior vice president would turn to me and ask me to quote the policy, and I did—adding the page number. I also memorized every store number, every department number, every store manager's name, and every phone number for every store, and by this time we had some three hundred stores or so. Though I did not realize it, I had become very valuable to Target, both for my creativity and for my intellectual abilities. However, I continued to feel inadequate, or less than, because of my inadequate writing skills, and to a lesser degree, my speaking skills.

After all, I grew up in an environment where if one attempted to pronounce words correctly, he was labeled an Uncle Tom or other derogatory name that meant you really wanted to be white and you were ashamed of your blackness. As such, many African Americans mispronounced words so that we could fit into the crowd, not realizing that practice can make perfect even when mispronouncing words. Thus, I would occasionally pronounce words incorrectly, and of course it was a big deal to some, but others recognized a deeper and much broader intellect in me, just as the air force had years earlier.

I now understand that because African Americans were systematically socialized to dislike who they are, denied educational opportunities and forced to pretend that they were not intelligent lest they were beaten, many became what they feared most—which to a degree continues to influence too many African American's belief that they are less intelligent. In fact, research has shown that if given a choice, most minorities have a preference to be white primarily because they believe that whites have to endure less pain and can simply be themselves.

As a regional staff member, I was given the opportunity to participate in the executive interviewing processes; this was another life-altering experience. It was here that I lost my identity for a period of time. It was here that

I succumbed to the Target system and embraced its values for better and for worse. It's funny now, as I reflect, but I actually embraced Target's values so fervently that I became the individual that the senior executives recommended others model themselves after in the Midwest region and throughout the company. I had become a living example of the types of individuals they were seeking to promote because of my behavior, which mirrored the extreme conservative culture the leaders were creating.

I had many great wins as a regional staff member in terms of product growth. The greatest win was the electronic dartboard. I recall having to really challenge the buyers and replenishment team to get them to stock the dartboard in large quantities in my stores in Wisconsin. Eventually, the buyers gave in and shipped the quantity I requested to a couple districts, and the dartboards sold out almost overnight. The buyers, now believers, bought dartboards for all stores, and for a year, Target sold more electronic dartboards than any other retailer in the country. Suddenly, I had made another name for myself. Now I was a merchandiser and an operator. Add that to my ability to select people, and I had become even more valuable to the leaders at Target.

While I was in this role, the new president and CEO, Bob Ulrich, had access to me and asked me questions continually. For example, I recall being on a jet trip traveling to Boise, Idaho, and he asked my input regarding the return policy. At that time, Target would give refunds up to twenty-five dollars without a receipt, and Bob wanted to know my opinion about raising the no-receipt return policy to fifty dollars because customers were complaining. His position was to stand on the twenty-five-dollar policy. I argued that most people in America are honest and that the thieves will find a way to cheat the system no matter whether the cash refund policy is twenty-five dollars or a hundred dollars. Not long after that trip, the no-receipt return policy was adjusted to fifty dollars I believe and subsequently much more.

On a subsequent trip, I challenged Bob to highlight the many things that we do for the communities around the country, such as giving 10 percent of the pretax profits to nonprofit organizations. That was a big can of worms for Bob because he did not want the spotlight on Target for giving to nonprofit organizations; he was giving because he viewed the communities as partners, and he feared that Walmart might retaliate. Bob oftentimes asked, "Is Walmart doing it?" If they were not doing it, he did not wish to do it either, I suppose, because he believed that Target was not established enough to fight an all-out price and marketing war with Walmart. Also, he felt that giving to charities was an act of kindness and should not be commercialized. Well, it took a while, but about two years later, a big sign went up in the front of all Target stores shouting out how we helped the local communities. There were many other wins and challenges in this role, but let's move to the next position I held.

District Manager

Finally, my day came to interview with Bob Ulrich and the executive team for a district manager's position. I recall the interview explicitly because of Bob's behavior. During my experience at Target, I had learned that the executive team was always looking for the next big win. They were looking for something that they could champion to their peers, the board, and ultimately the store teams.

I arrived at Target's headquarters, located in City Center in downtown Minneapolis, about two hours early because I wanted to relax and prepare mentally for the interview. On the main floor, there was a bookstore—I believe it was a now defunct Borders bookstore. I walked into the bookstore looking for something that I could talk about during the interviews, something that was new and different. Because they all knew me from the test store and regional staff, I believed that the primary purpose of the interviews was to share their personal values and to ensure that I was aligned with them and their mission. However, I also knew that the most important reason for them interviewing me was to steal ideas, and they knew that I was a wealth of ideas. After shopping the Borders bookstore, I discovered several great ideas.

I came across a book titled *Service America*, by Karl Albrecht and Ron Zemke. This book was packed with great ideas and facts about successful service by some great companies. I bought the book and quickly jotted down some facts, but what caught and held my attention was the story about

Disney. I quickly read that chapter and became an expert on Disney service. When interviewing with the executive senior vice president of human resources, I presented him with the Disney story. I told him that our customers should become our guests and our employees should be titled team members. Additionally, I told him that we should dress casually in red and khaki and that all executives should dress like the store team when visiting stores.

That same year, he went to visit Disney. He was there for a month to learn as much as he could about their service operation. The next year, Target was transformed into the fast-fun-friendly stores. The team members were dressed in red and khaki, and all executives wore red and khaki when visiting stores. I never received any verbal or written credit for the idea, but I knew where the executive senior vice president of human resources received that information. He was recognized as a star, not only at Target but nationally among his peers.

After he launched the idea that I presented to him for service improvements, Target went on to enjoy several record-breaking sales and profit years. That was not the last time that I offered an idea that changed the direction of Target while I made less than my peers and did not achieve the promotion that many of my peers had received. In fact, prior to leaving Target, I learned that I made as much as forty thousand dollars less than some of my peers, many of whom had half the responsibility I did.

The interview with Bob was brief, and I walked away a bit confused. During the interview I was asked why I thought I deserved to be a district manager and why I thought that I was qualified. My response was brief. I simply stated that I had performed at a level that exceeded that of my peers and that I had the support of my peers. Bob appeared to be a bit taken aback by my answer, and I recall his response: "You know, there is no going back. It's either up or out." I left that encounter with Bob with a very uncomfortable feeling that he was not supportive of moving me into a district-manager-level position. Once again, I felt that someone was placing a limit or cap on my future growth potential, and it did not feel good.

Soon after the interviews my supervisor, the senior vice president for what was termed region 100, initially told me that I was to be the district manager in Denver, which was very exciting to my family, but a day before I was to report, he changed his mind, and I was told that I was to report to Milwaukee, Wisconsin, as the district manager. I was very dejected because Milwaukee was known as the armpit of the organization.

I learned very quickly that the decision was altered because my supervisor's girlfriend, another regional staff member, was approved to be a district manager, and she refused to move to Milwaukee. As such, I was forced to move to Milwaukee.

My wife hated it the year and a half that we were there. However, it proved to be very beneficial for the company and for me. It was in Milwaukee, Wisconsin, that I displayed my best leadership skills; it was there that I taught Target once again how to fight and compete against Walmart and win big.

The Milwaukee market was struggling to survive because of high shrink and extremely high employee turnover. The market had become Target's clearance center, and that strategy was destroying the market. We had several stores in predominantly African American neighborhoods, and they had no financial growth for several reasons. First, those stores carried the same product that the stores in the more affluent suburban areas carried.

Second, the employees were expected to conform to the same attendance standards as all stores, with no flexibility. However, because of the challenging weather in Milwaukee and because African Americans relied primarily on public transportation, holding them to strict times proved to be problematic. Given those facts, we held standards, but because of the transportation challenges, we made them somewhat flexible. With just a small adjustment in the scheduling process that allowed some flexibility regarding start times, the strangest thing happened. The employees began to take more ownership of their schedules, and if they were going to be late, they would call and ask other employees to cover for them until they arrived.

However, the most significant and meaningful change in those stores was the almost complete elimination of call-offs or no-shows. Turnover was reduced, and productivity improved significantly; sales and profits started to turn positive as well. Additionally, we challenged our marketing partners to bring in products that African Americans wanted to buy and remove those items that were of no value to their families which they did not purchase.

With these changes, sales continued to improve, and shrink was reduced significantly.

I also found that while the Milwaukee community loved bargains, they did not wish to be considered a community of people who wanted clearance merchandise. After many arguments with the regional staff and buying office, I convinced them that we needed a new go-to market strategy in Milwaukee, and I finally earned their support. We brought quality upscale merchandise into our suburban stores, just like the Target stores in Minneapolis, and sales really took off. There were additional benefits as well. For example, the employees became more committed to the stores and started to maintain the stores better. In fact, the stores looked like real Target stores.

The stores continued to improve so quickly that my supervisor visited the market twice while I was there. He came alone once because he wanted to understand, without interruption, exactly what I had done to turn the market around so quickly.

Small-Market and War Strategy

Because of my previous success as a store manager and a regional staff member and my great success in Milwaukee, my supervisor, with the support of the board, decided to launch a new market strategy under my leadership in Wisconsin. They wanted to completely differentiate this new store format from our traditional stores and from Walmart. Yet they wanted to compete with Walmart on what was considered Walmart's turf in rural Wisconsin. The Wisconsin market would expand into the Fox Valley area, and eventually throughout northern Wisconsin, adding eight stores, I believe. This was where we would fight Walmart with our small-market strategy on their challenging turf. It was not easy, but we were successful, and we learned a tremendous amount from this experience.

The war with Walmart started after we opened three stores in the Fox Valley area, one next to a Walmart store. In fact, one of our stores shared the same parking lot with a Walmart store. During this period, Walmart had their store manager shop Target for the major sale items, and they would display the same items in a basket at the front of their stores comparing the price difference. The price difference could be substantial, as much as 30 percent. One day, I decided to complete a price check at Walmart on main items that were on sale in our store. That day an employee from Walmart purchased the sale items from our store and set up a shopping cart in front of their store for comparison. However, their scheme involved buying our sale items and then going back to their store to mark these same items down far below our sale prices. After they had lowered their prices, they placed large signs on the carts shouting out the price difference. Of course, this made us look very expensive to the consumers. Additionally, reducing their prices of the same or similar items after purchasing them from us during our sale to mark the items below their regular and sale prices was ethically wrong.

After learning of this deceitful practice, I invited our CEO to visit so I could review with him the dishonest tactics Walmart store managers were doing to compare their prices to our prices. I also wanted to reintroduce him to the war strategy that had become an integrated part of the way Target conducted business, although the executive vice president of marketing and merchandising did peel back some of the strategy, which proved to be very damaging to Target in terms of sales and profit in recent years.

I recall that the CEO became extremely angry after seeing for himself what Walmart store managers were doing regarding comparing prices to Target's. He was shouting as he walked to the corporate jet, "I am going to sue those SOBs." Well, it turned out that this was an issue throughout the country. Target did file a lawsuit, and eventually that practice by Walmart stopped. I have no idea if the Walmart executive team was complicit in this underhanded, unethical scheme, but it finally stopped.

After this incident and after the CEO learned more about our war strategy, he commissioned an external organization to visit stores and to engage the store teams in brainstorming sessions to determine how the team members themselves would suggest we compete against Walmart going forward. The end results were as follows:

1. Store managers were given autonomy to price up to five hundred items competitively and to remain within 10 percent of Walmart on all key items.
2. Store managers in northern Wisconsin were allowed to host local community events in their parking lots.
3. The store managers were given a fun budget to buy food for employees.
4. Stores were remerchandised to some degree to reflect the desires of the community.
5. Stores were given additional training dollars to cross-train all employees to work in several departments.

This was the same strategy I had employed in Colorado, and once again the strategy proved to be extremely successful. In fact, these strategies, with the exception of allowing events in the parking lots, were rolled out to all stores coast to coast, and now Target was competing effectively against their nemesis, Walmart.

We proved to be so successful and competitive versus Walmart in the Fox Valley and northern Wisconsin markets that the CEO determined to open several more stores in northern Wisconsin, and they were successful as well. In fact, because of my creative and out-of-the-box thinking, we created several new marketing strategies that helped to situate Target far ahead of the competition. For example, we developed a manual bridal register that became an electronic registry and a national hit for most every major retailer. We also proved that items such as electronic dartboards had a home at Target. In addition, we started the bathroom checklist that is now a basic part of almost every public restroom in America.

Finally, after many successful initiatives that went global and proved to be important factors in the future success of Target, I was moved to Chicago as the district manager. I wondered why I was not offered the regional director's role. Even after performing at a level that no other district manager or executive in the organization had ever achieved, I was not promoted, and in fact, I would soon feel the debilitating sting of racism at Target.

These events lingered in my mind and eventually moved me to pursue my master's degree and PhD degree in an effort to discover some meaning and understanding regarding senior executives' decision-making processes for selecting senior-level direct reports. In fact, while working on my dissertation, I identified how and why the Target executives determined not to promote me to the director-level position until I threatened to quit. Stay tuned, because I will share the results of my dissertation research and some important information you need to understand in the decision-making process for selecting senior-level direct reports.

Regional Director and the KKK

Even after leading the effort to improve the value of the Target brand in Chicago, I was forced to demand a promotion (and threaten to leave if I did not get it) before I was honored with a director position. But that promotion did not come without serious backlashes—backlashes of racism and challenges that all but guaranteed an unsuccessful period in my life. As I reflect on that experience, I know that only one thing could have helped me through those most awful years of my life, and that was education. For the first time, I saw some white males turn their backs on me in support of an individual who we would later learn was not only racist but was found to be associated with the KKK.

Shortly after I was promoted to the regional director of stores in Chicago, my senior vice president was promoted to become the president of Mervyn's (then a subsidiary of Target) in the Bay Area. I continue to believe today that one reason he was promoted was because of all the success we had in Wisconsin and Chicago, and the board believed that he could take the same strategy to Mervyn's. His replacement, the vice president of operations and previously my supervisor for a very short period, where he exposed his tendency to be racist, proved to be my worst nightmare; this guy was worse than any extremist I have ever seen on TV, met in life, or read about. He simply hated all dark-skinned people, period.

Prior to this vice president of operations being named as a replacement for the senior vice president of our region, I was tagged as an outstanding performer, but within one year of his arrival, I was labeled as satisfactory. I recall that he was politically connected with the executive team at Target and an outstanding bullshitter, which the leadership team at Target loved. Though he was not a very bright individual, he came across as being a tough guy, displaying a behavioral style similar to our 43rd President George W. Bush and Donald Trump, and the leadership loved his bold behavior.

He always found reasons to challenge others aggressively to keep the focus off himself. This was one way that he could conceal his radical racist thoughts and behavior. However, I always noted that when we were with the team having cocktails, his focus shifted to me and to joking about African Americans. In fact, he oftentimes mocked southern black preachers.

Initially, I took it in jest, but his jokes became offensive, so I began to leave team outings early. I suppose that's what he expected would happen when he started his joke telling about African Americans. It's strange, but his behavior was identical to Donald Trump's degrading and ugly behavior toward all people but white males.

During that period of my life, I did not wish to use race as a defense, but in hindsight I would have been justified to do so. I spoke to the director of human resources, but he proved complicit and supportive of the behavior, and so nothing was ever done. I now realize that I should have sued him and Target for mental damages and for not promoting me. However, by now my younger daughter was doing great in her role in marketing at Target's headquarters, and I wanted to believe that not all of Target's executive team members were of that racist mind-set. As I reflect, however, I think I might have been wrong. There were many who exhibited racist tendencies, and later both my daughters experienced their biased behavior. Of course hindsight is always better, but the fact is that I should have revealed this dark side of the Target executive team during my tenure there, and that's one of my greatest regrets in life.

The very worst part of that horrible experience was when this racist senior vice president of our region, region 100, turned most of my team against me. He managed to convince them that I was not a worthy leader, and he told several of my direct reports individually that he would promote them if they helped him remove me from my position. Eventually he started to ignore me in meetings, and he rejected everything I said. Even worse, when I did present a compelling idea, he would give it to one of my peers to complete. Because he was well connected with the executives at headquarters, he was able to enlist the help of some senior leaders to support his efforts to remove me from my position.

In an effort to add more support for his racist reasoning to remove me from my director role in Chicago, he convinced the executive vice president of marketing and merchandising to support his efforts by visiting my most challenging Chicago city stores on Saturdays during the Christmas holiday season when I was away visiting stores in southern Illinois. Because of his negative behavior towards minorities I am convinced that this executive senior vice president of marketing, who later became the president of Target, at the very least sympathized with the radical and extremist KKK organization. Yes, he became the CEO of Target, but he was subsequently released because of his poor performance and results.

The regional senior vice president, whom I hesitate to call my supervisor, finally turned most of my team against me, and also many of my former supporters at headquarters. I recall meeting with the executive vice president of human resources, who said, "Well, Roy, it seems that you have allowed your whole team to turn against you." I immediately responded, "Larry, what can you do when your supervisor is leading the charge?" The regional senior vice president of our region continued to create lies about my performance, and frankly, after a while, I suppose the lies and pressure proved to be too heavy for me to bear, and my performance did slip.

Again, I can recall thinking that a well-rounded liberal arts education would have been a big help during this challenging time because my critical thinking ability might have been much more developed. Understanding human behavior or business politics could have made a big difference in the way I handled this situation. I had no business-savvy mentors at Target because the regional senior vice president that I had considered to be a supporter at the time was now with Mervyn's, and it seemed I was alone, with no support.

My greatest fears now were not being able to feed my family and the scary concern of being viewed as a failure. Even though I knew that something was seriously wrong in this situation—and I knew it was racism—I refused to tackle it head-on because I did not wish to be viewed as playing the race card and because of the other reasons I stated earlier regarding my daughters.

By now I was attending DePaul University, and I had developed a relationship with a professor, Dr. John Willets, who proved to be one of the mentors who helped me through these very dark and painful days. John helped me to realize that many of the issues I perceived as problems were very solvable. However, during those horrible degrading events led by the racist senior vice president for region 100 at Target, I was unable to identify alternatives because of my limited education, undeveloped critical decision-making skills, and lack of a strong and supportive mentor at Target and in my life. Thus, I was left in a state of mental distress.

Before I left Target, Dr. Willets convinced me to take one particular class at DePaul, a class that changed my view of education and changed my life. That was a critical-thinking class. In that class, John taught me how to identify the critical elements in any text—newspaper, magazines, books, reports—and in conversations. I was so enlightened by this class that I continued to take classes at DePaul University. With the knowledge from this single class and the support of John, and my best friend, Warren, I sorted through the decision-making process for determining my final steps regarding exiting Target and moving on with my life.

Leaving Target

After dealing with what I now know was a very unstable supervisor, someone who did not deserve a management title of any kind, I was a nervous wreck. I could barely sleep, and I would later learn that I had developed high blood pressure and that I experienced a mild stroke. I worked hard to keep this great pressure from my family because I wanted them to continue with a normal life and not lose focus on their happiness, joy, and careers. However, I am sure that they could see the pressure in my face and occasionally all over my body. I knew I had to make a decision regarding my future because my health was deteriorating fast. I also knew that I was slipping into a deep depression that

I could no longer control, and that was even scarier. For these reasons, I spent many hours on the phone and face-to-face with Dr. Willets; he eventually learned enough about the situation to explain to me his theoretical, scientific, and personal view of what was happening to me.

John preferred to stay away from the racism perspective, though we both had to come to grips with that possible conclusion eventually. John explained to me that my supervisor's interpretation of the world around him was not situated in realism. As such, he did not see me as deserving of the position that I held; he believed that I was evil and that I must be removed, even if he had to create an untrue story for others to believe, which he did. In fact, John explained that my supervisor's brain was so corrupted with hate and dislike for me that he viewed all of his statements toward me as being justified, and he viewed his harsh behavior as being correct because, to his mind, I represented the ugliness in his life, and he felt that it must be removed at all cost. Considering this, John recommended that I consider leaving Target.

The day I flew to Minneapolis for my final review with this guy that I no longer considered to be my supervisor, I knew, as the plane took off from O'Hara and landed in Minneapolis–Saint Paul, that that would be my last official day with Target. I remember the arrogance that this guy displayed as he read my review, a review that did not reflect the excellent results I had achieved in terms of developing talent, cleaning up messy stores in my region, and most importantly at that time, connecting with the city officials in Chicago. In fact, I recall participating in an event with Mayor Daley. He congratulated me on the great work I had done with the Target stores in Chicago and surprised me when he said, "I can't imagine how many whip marks you had to endure to get this position as director of stores at Target here in Chicago." Obviously, he was proud that I had endured what he knew must have been a very tough road to cross.

The review that the regional vice president read was all fabrication, and obviously I did not sign it. It was a very strange feeling walking out of the regional office that day; it was clear that he had informed everyone in the regional office regarding what he was about to do to me. I can laugh about that day now, but it was a very painful day at the time. It's funny that no one in the office would make eye contact with me, and my so-called friends were nowhere to be found. They had left for the day. I remember that he was dressed casually, with his overly tight black cowboy jeans and boots on and an ugly smirk on his face that would not last for long, but one that I will never forget.

It seemed that the one-hour flight back home was the longest flight ever. Though this guy had not asked me to leave the organization, I am sure he expected me to leave after receiving an average to below-average review. However, the one thing he underestimated was the importance of my relationship with Bob Ulrich and my relationship to Target.

The next day, a Friday, I returned to my office and e-mailed my resignation; I asked my assistant to box and ship my personal belongings to my house because I was done. I don't recall how I told my wife, but I do recall that she was very supportive. I am sure that she had seen the damaging effect that the job and the hostile behavior of the regional vice president was having on my life, and she was ready for me to leave. By Monday, things would take a different turn.

I was told by an insider that Bob the CEO of Target had previously made it clear to the human resources team that I was not to leave Target under any circumstances, period. In fact, he would only agree to giving me a reduced rating if human resources and my so-called supervisor guaranteed him that I would be brought back to lead a large district that was nearest his home in Minneapolis. I learned also that Bob said that if I left the organization, everyone associated with or involved in the decision to reduce my review or who caused me to leave would be fired. This was an indication that I was much more valuable to Target than this regional vice president realized and the human resources team had calculated.

At that time, I could not understand how I could be so valuable to Bob and the organization and not be qualified for a vice president position. I could not get the support of the executive team at Target because the regional senior vice president knew how the game was played at that level, and because of his political astuteness, he was accepted into the good ol' boys' club with open arms. It is ironic that in the end, Bob saw me as being more valuable than all the executives collectively who made the decision to lower my review and ultimately cause me to leave the organization, but he could not sign off on me moving to higher positions.

Because of my research during my work on my PhD, I now understand all the reasons for the unconditional support of individuals such as this racist regional senior vice president by other white male executives, even when he clearly did not deserve any support at all. Though I now understand the reasons why he was a racist and hater of individuals that dressed in a different fashion than he, I remained surprised that Bob Ulrich supported what was clearly unethical treatment of me after all that I had done for Target.

Now the regional senior vice president was under fire, and I had the upper hand. I turned in my resignation, and now Bob began to ask top executives at Target when I would return to work. Finally, I found some joy in this situation.

The regional vice president called me every other day for four weeks begging me just to return to work. He actually said, "You can remain in your current position. Just come back to work." He even offered to change the review and to make it more positive. I still refused to return because I now understood that he was unbalanced; his hatred for me and people who resembled my appearance was situated in racism and bigotry, and I would not be successful working with him in any capacity. After six weeks of him begging me to come back to work, we finally signed a separation agreement. Bob Ulrich told them to pay me for the six weeks that I did not work and to give me a separation package without any arguments or bickering.

In a few months and true to his word, Bob first fired the director of human resources for the region. Next, shockingly, he fired his friend, the executive vice president of human resources as well. The senior vice president of human resources, a white female, quit when I left after she told me in private conversation that if I left, she would leave, because it was clear that Target did not support diversity. It was a bit more challenging to remove the racist senior vice president of region 100 because he was an excellent politician and astute liar.

About six months after I left Target, I received a call from Darrell, one of my old friends and a store manager at Target in Minneapolis, and he shared some news that was extremely shocking and later proved to be true. While hosting a regional meeting with one hundred or so store managers and many staff members, the regional senior vice president made a shocking disclosure. During his speech, he stated his support for the KKK and the great work they had done for the South and for America. He made it sound as if the KKK had members in many parts of many organizations, including Target.

One day after this awful event, Darrell called me with the grim news, and my first response was, "That cannot be true." I asked if the regional senior vice president was still working, and he said yes. I was outraged that no one at Target had taken any action against this guy. This made it very clear to me that it was more important for these executives to protect individuals like themselves than to have creative minds on board who could move the organization forward.

During this same time frame, the former executive senior vice president of operations had recently returned from Mervyn's to become the executive senior vice president of operations at Target. I called him and made it clear that if the senior vice president for region 100 was not fired promptly, I would sue Target and take the news to every social activist in Chicago.

During this same conversation, the newly returned executive senior vice president of operations asked if I had received the restricted stock options he left for me. I explained that no one ever mentioned that I had restricted stock options. I later learned that the racist senior vice president who became my supervisor and the director of human resources cancelled my stock options on the first day that he became the senior vice president of the region, even though he had not worked with me for one single day during that review period. It is my understanding that those options are worth several hundred thousand dollars now. I can only assume that he assigned my well-earned stock options to someone of his choosing, someone who had accomplished very little in our region.

Several months later, that racist regional senior vice president was fired. I know now that the leadership team at Target was very much aware of his affiliation with, or at the very least, his love for the KKK, because it was easily confirmed from his Internet posts. I was shocked to learn one year later that he was the vice president of the West Coast region for a Fortune 500 office supply company, and I believe he remains there today.

It's ironic that I was interviewed and asked to join this office supply company as a regional vice president for the Chicago and Hawaii region. However, when I realized that the racist former Target senior vice president was a vice president with the organization, I turned down the position. The executive vice president of operations and the president for this company both asked me why I turned down such an outstanding offer, and I simply stated that I would not work with the former regional senior vice president of Target, period. They offered me additional salary and bonus and said, "You will be his peer, so what can he do to you?" I refused because I knew that he was associated with the KKK, or at the very least, that he was a supporter. In fact, if I gave you his name and you Googled this former senior vice president of Target, you would pull up the egregious statements about minorities that this guy wrote some years back.

Though I did not expose him during my interview with the office supply Fortune 500 company, I did ask questions of the human resource lead and the VP of diversity that should have given them clues as to his affiliations with the KKK. I asked how many district managers or directors of color worked for him out west, and I was not surprised when I was told none. The VP for diversity went on to say, "Every time we place an African American or Latino in his region, they leave after a few short months." I am hopeful that this organization will deal with him because the future growth of their organization will depend on a diverse team. I am also hopeful that Target's new leaders understand the value of diversity and inclusion in relation to creativity, sales, and profit for Target's long-term future. Obviously, looking back, I wish I had exposed this unstable individual and sued Target to hell and back.

CLASS-ACTION LAWSUIT

Recovering from the racist treatment that was delivered at the hands of a self-proclaimed KKK lover was a real challenge. Though I had experienced racism and biased treatment almost daily for much of my adult life, the brutal, in-your-face racism delivered by that guy proved to be extremely damaging to my health, both physically and mentally. Ironically, I had the opportunity to damage Target's reputation because of a class-action lawsuit alleging discriminatory practices at Target.

A few months after they fired the racist regional vice president that was my former supervisor, I received several calls from Target's legal department that I did not return. Eventually, the leadership was under such pressure from their legal team that they had someone that I had marginal respect for call me, the now executive senior vice president of operations and my former supervisor before the racist began calling me.

Though I had recently found that the executive vice president of operations was really a part of the good ol' boys' regime at Target, I still had some respect for him. Begging, he requested that I give a deposition on Target's behalf. At the same time, the group leading the class-action lawsuit requested that I support their claim that Target was a racist organization that discriminated against minorities. I was conflicted and confused regarding which path to take for several reasons. First, I was mentally drained and simply did not have the energy to fight in either direction. Second, the separation package I signed with Target had language in it that restricted what I could say about the organization. Finally, as stated previously, my younger daughter was now employed at Target and doing extremely well, and my elder daughter was considering joining Target, which she eventually did. As angry as I was with Target, I still wanted to believe that there were some decent people in the organization and that they would be fair to my daughters. As such, I decided to support Target. Obviously, today I realize that that decision was not in my own best interests or the best interests of my daughters and other minorities at Target.

There were two areas that the plaintiffs were exploring, and both centered on me. If the legal team representing the plaintiffs could have gotten me to confirm either allegation, Target would have been in big trouble, costing them untold millions of dollars in business and talent.

First, they wanted to confirm that I was the only person at Target supporting diversity. Their premise for this was the fact that I mentored virtually every minority manager or executive in the organization from coast to coast, and there were approximately two hundred at the time, including store management individuals, both women and men. Second, they wanted to confirm that I had evidence to support their findings that some of Target's language was coded to discriminate against minorities. I found myself struggling to support Target. As such, I was not a very good witness for them, because, in fact, both arguments were true.

The attorney representing the lawsuit spent four hours asking me one question in several different ways, and I remember doing everything possible to avoid answering her question. She asked, "How many minorities, meaning blacks, Latinos, and women, did you mentor at Target?"

My response was, "I don't recall."

She said, "Was it one hundred, two hundred, three hundred, or more, Mr. Whitmore?"

I said, "I don't recall."

She continued, saying, "You must have some idea, Mr. Whitmore." She asked the same question again, and she finally said, "Mr. Whitmore, this is a legal proceeding, and you are withholding evidence. You will be held in contempt if you do not respond."

At that time Target's attorney stepped in and said, "If you do not stop badgering our witness, we are going to walk." He then requested a break.

That afternoon, the attorney representing the plaintiffs moved into her second phase of questioning. This line of questioning centered on Target's interviewing process. Though I was not a senior executive, she was well aware that I led many of the interviews for new management hires at every level at Target. She was also aware that most internal managers who were promoted had to interview with me as well. However, she was most interested in the group interviews and some of the words used to describe minorities that did not fit Target's image for being a leader. The primary word they used was "perception." In virtually every interview of a minority, particularly an African American, most of the white interviewers, almost to a person, labeled the individual as "lacking perception" or "missing the big picture" or both. If one could uncover the old interview notes, they would reveal, with a high degree of consistency, that their responses did indeed support the premise of the lawsuit. In fact, even when the interviewers signed off for a minority to be promoted or to join the organization, they usually did so with the reservation that the minority candidate lacked perception and the ability to see the big picture.

At that time, I knew something was wrong, but I did not know how to explain it; I did not have the knowledge to grasp what they meant by "perception" or "missing the big picture." When I asked the white interviewers to explain the meaning, they had great difficulty doing so. Eventually, I became concerned that if I continued to ask them to explain what they meant by "lack of perception," they would label me as lacking perception and not having the capacity to see the big picture—whatever the hell the big picture was. In fact, I am sure that somewhere in my records, you could find a statement that said Roy Whitmore was "lacking perception and could not see the big picture."

Again during this line of questioning, I stood fast and protected Target for the reasons I previously stated, but mostly to protect my daughters. The attorneys that filed the lawsuit dropped it after they could not convince me to support their case. However, based on Target's history after I left it is clear that it was wrong for me not to join the lawsuit against them.

It was ironic that about a year after my elder daughter was hired at Target, she called me, upset, and said that she had just come out of her interview, in which she was labeled as lacking perception. By now, I had completed my undergraduate work, and I was well on my way to completing my first master's degree. Now I was mentally prepared to deal with this crazy situation head-on; even though I was steaming with anger, I knew what steps to take.

When working on my master's degree at DePaul University, I studied the psychological testing that Target used to confirm their so-called perception label. I learned that their assessment was flawed because the results were generally interpreted and verified by one individual; furthermore, the evaluation was designed using research that only captured the thinking and behavior of white male executives. This assessment was not intended to assess the cognitive capabilities of minorities. Because minorities frequently have different experiences in life, their responses to some of the questions might appear to be strange or wrong, when in fact, their responses could offer a creative advantage to an organization. Again, the results of these assessments always showed that the minorities lacked perception. I was angry and now well prepared to engage Target about this insane conversation at a broad and profound level.

The very next day, I called the executive senior vice president of operations and the legal team at Target, and I was very direct in my language. I stated, "My daughter just received her year-end review, and she is upset because she was labeled as lacking perception. While I might have accepted that nonsense for some folks in the past, now it is very clear to me that because minorities do not articulate or see through the lens you expect them to, they are labeled as lacking perception. I also might accept this if my daughter was not probably the smartest person at Target. Every SAT, college intro exam, or psychological exam she has taken has clearly identified her in the genius range in terms of intelligence. So your old biased team selected the wrong minority person to label as lacking perception. If you do not stop using that term to label minorities in your attempt to exclude them from your organization and higher positions today, I will personally gather signatures and file a class-action lawsuit that will destroy Target."

I never mentioned to my daughter that I had engaged Target, and she never again mentioned that they used those words to define her intellect or abilities. I never wanted my daughters to think that I intervened on their behalf, because they are pretty independent, smart, and very capable of taking care of themselves. However, I did not wish for them to be distracted by craziness; they should be able to perform at their best every day, just as others are allowed to do.

As you can see, corporate life is a challenge for black males and oftentimes for black females, as well. There are documented reasons of biased treatment of blacks in corporate America by the mostly white C-suite executives, and all are situated in false beliefs that have been passed down in the executive suite for more than two centuries. Many of their beliefs about minorities are so ridiculous that just a simple questioning of their belief will prove the opposite. For example, the myth that blacks are lazy, rapists, and thieves was created by white plantation owners to keep the North from fighting to end slavery much earlier. In fact, these lies were pushed even harder after slavery ended to keep the northern whites from hiring blacks, so blacks would have to become sharecroppers. In this situation, to obtain work, many blacks had to migrate back to the South to work in the fields and be house servants. During this period, the South instituted the Jim Crow era to ensure that their racist verbiage would stick to African Americans—for eternity.

Now I ask you to consider this simple question: How can one be lazy when he or she works from sunup to sundown six or seven days a week picking cotton and tobacco and cleaning plantation homes? Being lazy simply does not fit with working ten- to twelve-hour days, six to seven days a week. Those who peddled these lies should have been challenged, and these lies should have died. However, they did not, and many whites and blacks have come to believe these myths, and they allow these lies to control their beliefs about others. In fact, brothers, too many of you have come to believe these lies about yourselves, and for far too many years now, you have been living down to these awful standards.

Lesson 4: Faith in Your Life

You must have faith in God first, then your family and fellow brothers; start now to develop that faith. Many times, a major event will help us to realize our true calling and develop a deep, unyielding, and unbreakable faith in ourselves. I spoke about the event that changed my life and helped me to strengthen my faith in my abilities and in my future: when my mom had to serve my dad and me through the back door of the family's home that she cleaned. On that day I suddenly grew up. I no longer cared about being a gang member. I cared about changing the picture I saw that day. I recall developing a thought that never left me, one that I continue to recite today: "Why can't I?"

Why can't I own the home of my desires? Why can't I have the job or position of my desires? Why can't I have the money that I desire? Why can't I have the education that I desire? Why can't I feed the homeless and the hungry? Yes, I have been able to do all of these things, and I am not done yet.

Developing a deep faith in self is not easy, but it starts by developing a deep faith in God. I am most certainly not perfect, but I really try hard to maintain a deep faith and belief about the things I desire. Your faith in God, self, and family must be unwavering. And let me give you a bit of advice: as you develop this deep faith, be careful not to share it with others until your faith is so strong that even Satan himself could not affect or influence your belief.

It was by faith that I have achieved a vice president position; it was by faith that I obtained two master's degrees and a PhD from very good schools. It will be difficult to develop this unwavering faith in yourself, but you must start believing now. Your future is filled with promise, but you must develop the faith to go get it. What's scheduled for you in the future is only for you, and you can't have it if you don't have great faith in your desires and the dreams that God has placed in your heart. See yourself embracing that which you desire and deserve—and don't let go.

Deep faith works best with a written plan. Develop your plan today, because tomorrow could be too late. What are your desires? Write them down on white paper with blue lines…I don't know why, but one of my professors told me that when you write down the things you desire on white paper with blue lines and look at them every day and visualize yourself as having them, through great faith you will obtain them. In fact, I have been practicing this for many years now, and I can confirm that it works, but you must have great, unwavering faith in your desires coming true. This faith development process is not easy, but to become all that you should be, you must practice faith building, now and forever.

> Faith is a living, daring confidence in God's grace, so sure and certain that a man could stake his life on it a thousand times.
>
> —MARTIN LUTHER

CHAPTER 5

From Target to Jewel-Osco

AFTER LEAVING TARGET, I was bombed and in a deep fog. My wife and I first determined to get away for a while, and so we rented a cabin in the forest about fifty miles from home for a few days. This was a wonderful getaway because we had no phone and no TV; we could only watch a video recorder. After that, we determined to take a trip to Saint Lucia, and this is when I learned that I had developed high blood pressure. Prior to the trip, I developed a sinus infection and wanted some medicine to ease the pressure so I could fly in some comfort. The doctor refused to give me antihistamines because I had high blood pressure. I had recently experienced some of the extreme pressures that African Americans deal with, and now some of the reasons that we develop this life-threatening illness were becoming clear to me.

After a month, I began to seriously search for a job; however, I was not healthy, not only due to high blood pressure, but because I was still mentally exhausted, and I could not think clearly or rationally. I now understand that the relentless racist treatment that I received at Target had caused me to develop irrational and dysfunctional thoughts that made me a nervous wreck. I rarely slept, and almost everything frightened me. A loud knock at the door would cause me to shake internally. I think I hid these very scary and uncomfortable feelings from my family fairly well. I eventually slipped into a deep depression, which was most difficult to recover from. However, as I stated earlier, with the help of Dr. Willets, my mentor and friend, I eventually improved.

The Limited Corporation

After a couple months of mental recovery, I obtained a job with the Limited Corporation as the director of operations for their Structure brand, which is no longer around. The promise was for a vice president role to replace the current individual, who was not doing well. However, after thirty days, the individual I was hired to replace was still on board, and he was beginning to become very difficult. Flashbacks of Target days were creeping into my mind, and I was not mentally ready to deal with him after the horrible ordeal at Target. I found his behavior to be similar to that of many of the individuals I worked with at Target; as such, I left and returned their $30,000 sign-on bonus, which I had never cashed.

Jewel-Osco

Previously, while at Target, I met the vice president of human resources for Jewel-Osco at a conference sponsored by Mayor Daley, where we were presenting. She told me after the event that if I ever left Target, to call her, and she would be happy to bring me on board as a vice president for operations. After several months, Kathy and I were presenting at another conference, when she learned that I had left Target. After the conference, she immediately called and invited me to Jewel-Osco for an interview. During the interview, I met the president, Gregg, and many other executives, and I was pleased with their authentic down to earth behavior. Though I did not particularly care for the food business, I felt comfortable with the team, and eventually, they made me an offer to come on board in a training position to learn the grocery business, with the promise of a vice president position; I accepted.

By now I was much stronger mentally, and I had completed my undergraduate degree and much of my graduate work at DePaul University. There was no doubt in my mind that because of my previous experiences at Target and my formal education, I would quickly find success at Jewel-Osco. The training lasted for nine months; now I was halfway through my master's program and much more astute regarding human behavior. I was intellectually stronger in the financial aspects of the profit and loss statement, as well as marketing strategy. In fact, I could now apply various human development theories and mathematical equations along with my previous experience to help me solve issues at work. It was fun now because I had fully developed my critical thinking abilities.

I went in as a district manager in training for nine months, but I had to complete all the various roles, which included department manager, store manager, and finally district manager before I was promoted to a regional vice president of operations in the north area. The training process was fun. I enjoyed my experience in the bakery. I loved interacting with the long-term employees, and I found their dedication to Jewel-Osco to be second to none. It was just like a family, and they loved the organization.

After working at Target, I was surprised at how excited everyone at Jewel-Osco was to simply be an employee in the organization. Most did not care about promotions. They were simply happy to have a job at the largest and most recognized grocery chain in the Chicago area. At Target, everyone wanted to be promoted. Being promotable was an implicit part of Target's atmosphere, particularly for managers and executives. In fact, if one found oneself not promotable, one would soon be out of Target.

After nine months, I was promoted to a store manager for exactly one week, and promptly promoted to a district manager position for thirty days, and then to a regional vice president for the north region. My being assigned the north region was a shock to many because it consisted of the suburbs of Chicago, which were predominantly white. The senior VP of operations at that time, Keith, was particularly upset because he wanted one of his buddies and cronies to have the north area. However, the current president Gregg and the human resources team would have none of that. They knew that it was time to take a stand and force diversity into the north region of Jewel-Osco.

Of course, all eyes were on the north region and me. Yes, I did perform by improving all the financials and the pharmacy operation. I promoted more talent than the other two regions, and similar to Target, I developed a war strategy for Jewel-Osco to fight Walmart, although it was never implemented completely by the senior vice president of operations until the long-term

Jewel-Osco leaders left. The north region had previously been a very good region, but now it was the star of the entire company coast to coast.

Keith's Promotion—and I Went South

We had staff meetings every Tuesday morning at 7:30 a.m. sharp, and on one particular morning, I knew something was going on because the corporate executive vice president and human resources leader were in the meeting. Sure enough, they delivered some news that shocked me to my core…news that frankly few in the meeting except Keith could accept. The executive vice president announced that Keith was the new president of Jewel-Osco. My peer and I were shocked, and we both knew that our lives would change.

Previously, I had been promised the senior vice president position in the Chicago region when that position opened. However, the same day that Keith was promoted, he delivered two pieces of news that forced me to rethink my future once again. He told me via the phone that the company was moving in a different direction and that I would not be considered for the senior vice president position. Later that same day, he asked me to come by his office, at which time, proudly, with a smile on his face, he told me that I would be moving to the south region. I was obviously disappointed, but now I was intellectually stronger, and I had been through a similar situation previously…I was prepared to fight the good fight both politically and intellectually. I would not make it easy for Keith.

Keith looked for any negatives that he could in my performance, presentations, and results. He did not think that I was a good fit for operations because I did not scream and belittle employees as he and his supporters did. He looked for, and in fact he created, negative issues about me that did not exist. I now understand that he was using heuristics to confirm his false beliefs about me, but I was prepared for the political and racist fight now if I needed to fight. I had experience and education on my side now, and with that, I was a formidable foe for any situation that I encountered.

I took over the south area from Bob, one of Keith's best friends, and I quickly learned that the region was a mess. Bob had come to believe, like too many, the myth that stores located in predominantly African American communities were not expected to perform as well as those located in the suburban areas. I quickly put that myth to rest. Within one year, the performance of the stores located in the south region was better than those located in the north—an unexpected turnaround. Keith had expected that I would fall on my face, and then he would be able to say, "I told you so."

Not long after Keith became the president of Jewel-Osco, I started to work on my PhD, and I slowly began to lose interest in working with individuals who had little clue about human behavior or how to effectively motivate employees. Although I lost interest, I was leading and managing at a very high level. In fact, the financial numbers continued to improve versus the region and company. It was during this time that I began to plan my exit strategy from Jewel-Osco. This was, of course, before the big market crash.

My last year at Jewel-Osco was really fun because I was well prepared. My previous experience, and most importantly my education, helped me think critically and make better decisions faster. Thus, I was very comfortable in meetings now and in presentations. However, my greatest win in my last year at Jewel-Osco was building a winning team. I took a team that many viewed as being average at best and made them into shining stars. In fact, more team members were promoted from the south area than the other two areas combined.

The last year was fun for other reasons, as well. By now Keith had accepted the fact that I was an excellent leader, and he started to seek my advice on many important business matters. I was surprised in one meeting when he turned to me and said, "You don't think I am very smart, do you?" I never explored this statement beyond that day, but I did attempt to ensure that I was not using my education to make him uncomfortable.

I was considerate enough to give Keith a thirty-day notice, and I was pleasantly surprised, again, when on several occasions, both Keith and the human resources VP asked me to stay on. I was pleased that Keith gave me a big party, spending at least several thousand dollars. I knew then that he had developed more respect for me than he ever shared verbally or demonstrated in his behavior toward me. However, by then, I was so turned off by corporate politics in retail that I simply wanted to do something different: I wanted to run my own business.

Thus, I purchased a recruiting franchise from Global Recruiting Network (GRN), investing some $150,000 plus the cost of living over a two-year period, and the return on investment was minimal. This proved to be a poor financial investment, and the financial meltdown made the decision look even worse.

The Monday after I left Jewel-Osco, the stock market went into a free fall…I was in shock as I watched my savings disappear. I was losing $5,000 to $10,000 an hour, and my financial adviser would not return my calls. He did not move my money until I eventually threatened to fly to his office in Phoenix, and by then I had lost more than $200,000. To make things even more concerning, my Supervalu and Albertson's stock options were in a free fall and dropping just as fast. I had planned to pay cash for my Ph.D. studies with my Albertson's stock, but that option was off the table now.

I was deep into my Ph.D. studies, and dropping my studies was not an option. I could not bear the thought of walking away, having invested money and time, with no degree; I had to complete my Ph.D., and even at that point, somehow I knew that completing my Ph.D. was the right thing to do—not just for me, but for my family. I would be the first ever in my family to earn a Ph.D. I knew that as costly as this Ph.D. was in terms of time and money, it was worth it because of the confidence that it would build in future generations. In fact, I believe that because of my commitment to education, both my daughters returned to college to complete their master's degrees. I think that to some extent they were inspired by my educational efforts to improve their education and that, in and of itself, was worth all the hard work indeed.

LESSON 5: EDUCATION IN YOUR LIFE

In the previous chapters, there have been two consistent messages, and they are education and God. In the early years of my life and professional career, education was the key that I either missed in critical situations or that assisted me in a big way through some challenging crises. Yes, education is the great equalizer. As an African American male, you must do three things to at least give yourself a chance to change the way too many Americans view you and to a great degree the way you view yourself.

First, you must read and understand our Constitution and all the amendments, but start with the Declaration of Independence.

Second, you must vote in every election. You must start today to teach all of your children, relatives, and friends the importance of voting. Voting the right people into office can change your life and your children's lives. Voting is a right that you simply must exercise, and not just in national elections; in fact, it's more important that you vote in local elections because that's where the vast majority of the laws and leaders that have some influence in your life are created. The individuals that you put in local offices will govern your communities and can change your life. These are the mayors, the judges, the attorneys general, city council people, and much more.

Like you, I am angry when I see our young men shot in cold blood by white police officers, or any police officer, for no good reason at all, but I am equally as angry when I learn that a community is mostly black, and the black community did not get out and vote. In the coming chapters, I will tell you why it is crucial that you teach your kids the importance of voting—not tomorrow, but today. In recent years the US Census Bureau data suggest that of the eligible African American Voters, 73 percent were registered, and 66 percent of the registered voters voted in the 2012 presidential election. We must do better if we wish to have a meaningful voice in America's future in the coming years. Folks, it is OK to protest, scream, and yell, but please understand that it is more important to vote…please, please vote.

Remember and understand that education is the great equalizer. You can indeed change your life and the world about you through education. I know that our education system is broken from a financial perspective, and in some cases, the education that you might receive is less than adequate, but any education is better than no education. As difficult as it is for me to say this, take the financial aid and get your education, for with an education you will give yourself the opportunity to earn enough to repay your loans. In fact, just recently, recent studies indicated that almost all the jobs made available since the financial crash in 2008 were filled by individuals with a college degree.

It is through education that you will come to better understand the world about you, our economic system, our capitalistic system, our legal system, and our religious systems. You will learn how to better operate in our social system and to know when you are out of step with our various systems. The best way to grow in our social system is to first understand its guiding principles.

Finally, keep God in your life. Throughout all my life challenges, I have worked hard to maintain faith in my God. I want you to know that there is a higher power, no matter what name you wish to attach to him, her, or it. There are powerful positive forces that can guide you through life's challenging situations…but you must believe.

> Education is the most powerful weapon which you can use to change the world.
>
> —Nelson Mandela

CHAPTER 6

PhD Journey

EVEN AS I SLIPPED INTO somewhat of a panic mode because of the loss of much of my financial wealth, I knew that I was doing the right thing in pursuing my PhD. Somehow I knew that my faith in God and my critical thinking ability developed through education would get me through—and they have. Also, the voice of my wife saying, "Maybe this is where you should be right now," helped me through the difficult days.

What I did not know was that the next five years would be the most challenging of my life because of two new events. First, I underestimated the challenge of obtaining a PhD. I did not understand how difficult it would be to develop new knowledge in a higher degree of learning. After all, I had been educated at one of the best universities in the nation, DePaul University, and I was, by all accounts, very creative. Second, I really underestimated the complexities of owning and operating my own business. These two dynamics once again placed a heavy stress and strain on my physical and emotional well-being.

For years as an executive at Target and Jewel-Osco, I had either one or two assistants helping me with the details of being an executive, and now I was alone. I was the secretary, accountant, human resources manager, and everything else that owning a small business required, and I was not very good at those jobs. I recall my elder daughter asking, "Dad, how are you going to manage without an assistant?" Actually, I found that I could not manage the workload of a PhD and operate a business alone effectively. For that reason, I hired an assistant, who was extremely valuable in the early days of my recruiting business with GRN.

Global Recruiting Network (GRN)

During the first week of training at GRN, I had an uneasy feeling about that organization—one that I had not felt previously. Deep down in my stomach, I knew that this was a bad investment. God was giving me a strong signal that I should walk away from this deal. However, at this point I believed that there was no turning back. In the weeks to come, I quickly learned that their system was a complex gimmick designed to get individuals to sign on to their franchise using their retirement funds. To be fair, there were a few successful franchise owners at GRN, but the vast majority failed in the first two years. Some of the challenges with GRN were the various fees. They not only received an initial investment up front of $50,000, but there was a monthly fee, and they collected 30 percent or so for each of the franchise's placements. I had to find a way out of this, because it was draining my savings and damaging my health.

Again, because of God's grace and blessing, I was able to make lemonade out of lemons. I was not building wealth, but I was able to support our lifestyle as I continued to work on my PhD. However, I found myself dipping into our savings far too often to support the business. Ironically, even as the markets crashed in 2008 and 2009, my best year in the recruiting business was 2009. I had a contract with Walmart that paid off handsomely, but the next two years were a challenge, as the business from Walmart dried up.

Eventually, I had to find a way out of my contract with GRN, and again God blessed me by sending a buyer my way. This individual purchased my business for $100,000. He paid $50,000 in cash and carried $50,000 as a loan. Without having, GRN involved I was able to focus on recruiting for myself without the burden of all the fees of being a franchise owner—fees that were paid with little reciprocal return. About six months after Jim purchased my business, he filed for bankruptcy. I knew the business would be a challenge for him, but I did not know that he would fail so quickly. For me, this was another confirmation that GRN was a fraud. Jim owes me $50,000 even today, which I am sure he will never repay.

The years following the sale of my franchise proved to be fairly good years for recruiting. I connected with an old friend from Target stores, Mary. Mary was now at Ross stores, and I was able to place eighteen managers and executives there, and that made a big difference in my lifestyle and my ability to stay focused on completing my PhD at Fielding Graduate University. Again because of God and education, I was able to figure out how to get on with my life from a positive perspective.

PhD Studies

My graduate degree at DePaul University was fun, and I expected my PhD studies at Fielding Graduate University to be, as well. However, I quickly learned that studying for a PhD was an intellectual level far above a master's degree. DePaul has superior professors, but I was now engaging with world-renowned professors at Fielding Graduate University—many of whom taught at universities such as Stanford, Southern Cal, the Naval Academy, and other well-known universities. I also underestimated the writing rigor for working on a PhD. It was extremely challenging.

My PhD journey was five and a half years of stress and pressure such as I had never experienced before. By day, my home office was about executive recruiting. By evening and night, it converted to a library, with research papers, books, and articles all over my desk and the floor. I was looking for small pieces of new information that had not been identified by any researcher previously.

When I entered my Ph.D. program, my focus was still on Target and a better understanding of how subordinates were selected. I wanted to understand why only certain individuals were generally selected for the C-suites or chief executive positions in Fortune 500 organizations. In fact, Sociologist David Embrick confirms in his article The Diversity Ideology in the Business World: A New Oppression for a New Age that nearly 97 percent of the C-suite executives in Fortune 500 companies were white males. This number was based on scientific research, not made-up numbers that companies submitted to the government—numbers that you would find when you searched the US Census.

C-suite executives are the individuals who make financial decisions for organizations. I needed to understand how it could be possible that 97 percent of these C-suite executives were white males when 51 percent of the population was female, 13 percent African American, and about 18 percent Latino and growing. Though I knew that racism and bias existed in the hiring process, somehow deep inside, I wanted to believe that this scary phenomenon had to be caused by more than bias, racism, or sexism. Finding the real answer proved to be a daunting challenge; the answer was very elusive.

After the submission of several proposals to my committee, one of my committee members challenged me to take the time to review my proposal in more detail, word by word. He argued that I would find the real answer in the first three chapters…and, yes, I did. A word that I was not familiar with came up consistently, and that word was the key to discovering the real answer to the question of how senior executives were selected for senior-level executive positions—and to completing my dissertation.

The one word that was consistent in my research was "heuristics," and while I had studied the definition during my research, I did not identify it as a contributor to the executive selection process. *Merriam-Webster* defines heuristics as a process for "involving or serving as an aid to learning, discovery, or problem-solving by experimental and especially trial-and-error methods <*heuristic* techniques> <a *heuristic* assumption>; *also*: of or relating to exploratory problem-solving techniques that utilize self-educating techniques (as the evaluation of feedback) to improve performance <a *heuristic* computer program>."

Herbert Simon, the father of heuristics and decision making, proposed that heuristics are methods for arriving at satisfactory solutions with modest amounts of computation, and humans seek to reduce the effort associated with the decision-making process. Thus, the title of my dissertation became *The Use of Heuristics by Senior Executives When Selecting Senior-Level Direct Reports*.

I began to obtain some clarity in the decision-making process for senior executives. In other words, senior executives, who are primarily white males, followed the same methods and approach for hiring senior executives in every situation. Even when their decision proved to be flawed, they reverted back to the same decision-making process and selected individuals who resembled them, arguing to themselves that they simply did not ask the individual who failed in their organization the right questions. Their intuitive belief was that the individual's profile was right, but they were not a fit because of teamwork or some other behavior attributes. They found it difficult to accept, or they could not admit to themselves, that they first selected individuals who most reflected them in appearance and behavior, and everything else was second.

Individuals at Target would say that regardless of experience, individuals who were talented and smart would be successful because they could figure out their leadership role. What they really meant was, if an individual was talented, smart, and not a minority, he or she could be successful. In some cases, they were correct because Target offered those who most resembled the individuals they considered to be successful all the support they needed to achieve success. Ironically, minorities were rarely ever "smart" because they could not see the "big picture." Sadly, I watched Target bring on smart and talented minorities and offer no support. What was more troubling was that when the new employee made even a simple mistake or did not behave as white males expected, the leadership quickly pointed a finger, saying something like, "I knew that she or he was not a good fit."

As I stated earlier, frankly I am still confused about the "big picture," although I realize now that this was a useful phrase for the hiring leaders to apply in their quest to reject minorities, because they did not need to articulate their position explicitly and implicitly. So, too, it was useful for maintaining a predominately white male leadership team. To support this premise, I offer the following: When I finally demanded that I be promoted to the regional director position for Target in Chicago, they did not fill the position that I held as the district manager for the first year. As a result, I was managing six district managers and a regional staff, and I was responsible for twelve of the largest stores in the market. That should never have happened, and frankly, it would not have happened for others.

Because of this rare finding, I was on my way to completing my dissertation, and ultimately my Ph.D. I had identified one of the reasons that the executive suite was 97 percent white male and why senior executives in Fortune 500 companies continuously hired individuals who looked like them. This remained true even though there was scientific and theoretical proof that organizations with a diverse executive team were more profitable for many reasons that this book does not have the capacity to engage. However, I continued to ponder this question and to conduct additional research, and I discovered implicit collusion among some C-suite executives that were pervasive and all but guaranteed that minorities and women were excluded from C-suite positions. Yes, it was something far more sinister. I'll discuss this further in a later chapter.

As I neared the end of this very challenging time in my life, I realized the importance of this educational process. I understood the important meaning of being the first in my family to complete a graduate degree; now I would be the first to complete my Ph.D. at an excellent and well-respected university among scholars—not Ivy League, but well respected throughout the world of education. I was on my way to becoming a doctor of philosophy, and that was a big deal. Now, even more determined to complete my Ph.D., I would push myself even harder.

The day finally came, and my family joined me in Washington, DC, for the ceremony. We were there for the week, and what a week it was. My best friends, Warren and Debbie, and Ben and Renay, also joined us for this exciting time in my life. Finally, my name was called, and I was anointed a doctor of philosophy. I gave a short speech that moved several of the faculty to ask to assist me with my autobiography. The book that you are reading now is a product of those discussions. This is that speech exactly as I wrote it.

Doctoral Graduation Speech
By
Roy Whitmore, PhD
Saturday, July 16, 2013 | Washington, DC

Thank you, Barbara.

First, thanks to my lovely wife for the sacrifices that she has made these last years. Thanks to my daughter Quendrida, for traveling here to be with me, and congratulations on completing your MBA at Texas

Woman's University. Thanks to Renay and Ben, my Minnesota family, for taking time to be here for this very special occasion. Thanks to my best friends, Warren and Debbie, for coming out to visit me. I acknowledge and thank my awesome committee members Barbara Mink for her unwavering commitment to excellence, and Keith Melville for his great support from the very beginning; thanks also to Mary McCall for sharing her vast wealth of knowledge with me, thanks to Terry Britton for keeping the facts straight for me, and finally thanks to Barbara Adams, my external reader, for offering her expert advice. [PAUSE]

More than fifty years later, I can recall vividly the words of a teacher when she asked me what I wanted to be when I grew up. Without hesitation I replied proudly, "I want to be a lawyer when I grow up." Well, just as quickly she replied, "Oh, that could never happen, Roy. The best you can ever hope to be is a trash collector, and if you tried really hard, maybe you could be a good electrician." Now there is nothing wrong with either; in fact, both are important to our health and our safety.

From that moment, I would not engage education with the same vigor…in fact, I would drift and become the leader of a gang…I only graduated high school because my mother would not accept less. I eventually grew tired of the gang life, and I determined to join the air force. For the first time I was labeled intelligent. In fact, the air force investigated my test results because they did not believe them to be true. Air force leaders later invited me to join the secret police team of the air force…I refused because I did not think I was smart enough. They then asked me to be an air traffic controller, but of course I could not help pilots land planes…heck, I had never been on a plane. Finally, I was offered the position of dental hygienist and medic… now, I could do that. However, I did not realize that I had to train to be an emergency room doctor for field duty…and that was hard.

I would leave the air force and in time become a regional director of stores and the operating VP for a large grocery store chain. I would turn the foretold trash collecting journey into an education journey and go on to obtain an undergraduate degree, two master's degrees, a master certificate in leadership, and now a PhD.

Yes, this unbelievable journey is true, but only because more people saw my worth than not, more people chose to help me than not, more people chose to love me than not.

Mahatma Gandhi reminds us when he says that

> "Every moment of your life is infinitely creative and the universe is endlessly bountiful. Just put forth a clear enough request, and everything your heart desires must come to you."

Lesson 6: Persistence in Life

For years a quote by Calvin Coolidge, the thirtieth president of the United States, inspired me to live my dream. Although I know that his belief was based on the life of a successful white man, still I have used this statement as a guiding light, and I recommend that you follow it with one addition, which I will explain later:

> Nothing in the world can take the place of persistence. Talent will not; nothing is more common than unsuccessful men with talent. Genius will not: unrewarded genius is almost a proverb. Education will not; the world is full of educated derelicts. Persistence and determination alone are omnipotent.

Yes, for years this was a guide for me and my life. I know that persistence is one of the keys to one's success. In fact, persistence alone can propel most white males to success in our great country for many reasons, and I offer just a few.

First, it was years after the US Supreme Court's 1953 landmark *Brown vs. Board of Education* decision giving African Americans equal rights to education before education in public schools improved. Now, juxtapose only having open access to education for the last sixty years or so with those who have had access to superior education for more than three hundred years. Second, consider the fact that many whites generally live in a cultural environment that consists of teachers, doctors, lawyers, and business leaders and owners, while African Americans are relegated to menial jobs or roles as cooks, butlers, and housekeepers. Tell me, who should have the advantage when it comes to intellectual ability? It is for these reasons that you must add education to your desire to be persistent in achieving your goals.

Remember that you are more than two hundred years behind the educational experience of the majority; as such, they can succeed on persistence alone, but in most cases, you cannot…you must, at all costs, educate yourselves, and you must educate your children and other family members. In chapter 8, I will reveal a very important reason for you to close the education gap as fast as you can.

Now with that said, I do agree that education without persistence is no good. Be persistent in chasing your dreams, and do not allow anyone's behavior or rhetoric to derail you. As I mentioned earlier, I was told by a guidance counselor that I could never expect to be more than a trash collector, and that I should be excited about that. Yes, she actually wanted me to be joyous about becoming a trash collector. She went on to say, "But if you try really hard, maybe you can become a good electrician." Without my mom, a few strong mentors, and several teachers who saw my promise, I might never have been persistent in going after my dream, my education.

Along with persistence and education, write down your goals and look at them every day of your life, and you will be amazed at how many you will achieve and how fast you will grow. As you may recall from lesson 4, one of my professors at DePaul University taught me this simple lesson. He told of how he had achieved every goal he set because he wrote them down on white paper with blue lines. He achieved his educational goals and financial goals, and he flew a World War II fighter jet—his greatest desire of all. Write your goals down, look at them, and do not share them with others, because too many people will apply their restrictions based on their limited belief system or their inabilities. Their restrictions or nonbelief will serve to distract you from the goals that you most desire. They will add such thoughts as

- But life is different.
- But real life…
- That's a big goal!
- Who is going to help you?
- Why do you think you can achieve those lofty goals?

And the doubt will go on and on; that's why I do not openly share my personal goals with anyone but my Father in heaven.

> First forget inspiration. Habit is more dependable. Habit will sustain you whether you're inspired or not. Habit will help you finish and polish your stories. Inspiration won't. Habit is persistence in practice.
>
> —Octavia E. Butler

CHAPTER 7

Our Social System

THIS CHAPTER IS VERY IMPORTANT, so please read it and reread it, because to truly understand our social system is personal power. Our social system is complex, complicated, and very dysfunctional. In fact, our social system is so complex that we have more theories to explain human behavior than one can count, understand, or identify. That's one of the reasons that we experience so much distrust and hate here in America. I initially considered reviewing some of the social science theories in this chapter, but I decided to keep it real, because this is for everyone and particularly for black boys. For far too long we have been praying for things to come that are only an illusion and never meant to be.

We have all been misled. We have been told things about our social system that were only real for the privileged ones, even when they were unworthy of some of the better things in life because of their incompetence. As such, you deserve to hear the truth as I see it through my eyes after many years of experience and education. I only wish I had been taught the truth about our social system much earlier in life. In this chapter, you will learn the social challenges that you will inevitably encounter in your life here in America.

SOCIALIZATION PROCESS FROM CHILDHOOD

For years I believed that Memphis and the South were the only places that African Americans were subjected to subpar education, medical care, and work opportunities, and it would be years before I was in the presence of some well-respected and successful African American men and women who understood our social system and had the compassion to share their knowledge with me and others.

I learned that the socialization process of African Americans was well designed, constructed, and implemented systematically in an effort to keep us subservient—primarily as the proletariat class of America, the working class. This systemic process to devalue African Americans in the eyes of all whites, and to a great degree the world, served two primary purposes. First, it confirmed in the minds of white Americans that African Americans were mentally incapable of performing jobs that required anything more than limited intellectual ability, but second, it also served to convince many African Americans that they were not very smart and really could not perform at the same level as whites in jobs that required a great deal of intellectual ability.

The leading cause for these negative beliefs regarding the intellectual ability of blacks was the lack of access to education for many years, at least until some sixty years ago. The fact that blacks had limited access to quality education after that served to reinforce in the minds of both the whites and blacks that African Americans had limited mental abilities, which is, of course, completely false. The sadness of this story is that most whites knew that African Americans were receiving a lower-quality education, oftentimes from unqualified teachers, yet they continued to blame African Americans for the intellectual differences.

It was as an adult with two degrees that I would finally understand how structured the system was that socialized blacks across America to become subservient and to lose the will to be creative and successful leaders and business owners.

I was at the Chicago Child Care Society, not far from the University of Chicago, near President Obama's home, giving a presentation about my life, along with ten other very successful African Americans, when I heard the same story from other individuals—many of whom grew up in every part of America. It was sad to finally learn and realize that we had all been fed the same sick, twisted input as kids from kindergarten through high school. What's even worse, many of us were told these stories by African American teachers and counselors. The story was consistent across America. We were all told that because we were black, we should only expect careers as trash collectors, city workers, or maybe electricians, and only if we tried really hard. Becoming a doctor, attorney, or professor was simply out of the question. I remain in shock even today as I write this book.

This socialization process was led by the politicians and leaders in most of the states in the South, and many of the northern states also bought into this craziness. California was the one and only exception. An education in California was generally the same for most kids, even during the so-called Jim Crow era.

It should be understood that the socialization process was not limited to our education system; it was woven into the fabric of every federal, state, and local institution in America. For many years, as African Americans, we really had little choice but to accept our role as servants, lest we be beaten, jailed, or fired. The craziest result of this horrible behavior was that some white males came to see this superior status as being their right and privilege. Even today, too many continue to believe that they have the right to treat African Americans inhumanely, and when we don't allow such behavior, their inability to accept us as equals causes them to come unwired. We are seeing much of that anger play out today due to the great hatred of President Obama.

My Perspective

First, I would like to review a book that every black boy should read. It is a book that explains best how we black boys were systematically conditioned to see through a corrupted lens of distrust and dislike for one another—how we were misled. This powerful conditioning process has caused far too many of us to fight and kill one another, when we should be loving and building one another up unconditionally. The next chapter will explain in more detail the importance of understanding our social system, but for now let's review our social system through the eyes of a black man.

The 110-page book *The Mis-Education of the Negro* offers the most comprehensive explanation of the socialization process of the Negro of any book I have read. There are many books that address America's social system and the systematic socialization process of African Americans, but Carter Godwin Woodson's book, originally published in 1933, is as relevant to African Americans' socialization process today as it was over eighty years ago. It's important that I highlight a few of his findings before we continue.

Black Americans are educated to desire the same things as white Americans but are denied the opportunity to obtain them at almost every level of their lives. Rather, in far too many organizations across our nation, they are forced to compete against one another for the one or two leadership positions they are allowed to access. In some states, black Americans cannot even obtain jobs as city street workers or trash collectors. Just visit Wisconsin and the city of Milwaukee to see the evidence. Consider the fact that Milwaukee is at least 27 percent black Americans, probably more, but if you drive the streets of that city, you will be hard pressed to see any blacks working in city jobs, period—not even as trash collectors.

During the miseducation of African Americans, we have been systematically trained and have learned to hold a very demeaning place in our social system. Because we have been educated to desire the same things as those in power but have been denied them categorically time and again in our plutocratic-led society, far too many of us have found our place of despair and unhappiness in ghettos created by them and maintained by African Americans. This is the place that some wealthy and misguided white men have learned to accept as the right place for African Americans, and their greatest desire is that these despicable places be maintained because they create fear in most of white America, and fear sells easily to the majority of the American population.

Through fear, these plutocrats can continue to build their wealth. Even today, much of the negative news on mainstream TV and cable, to a great degree, is focused on African American communities. The media sells negative news to uneducated whites because they buy products that are advertised on the stations that they support; the media cannot survive without selling hate to whites, lest the advertisers move their advertising dollars elsewhere. Thus, the media have become a great training ground for hate. Individuals like the mad Koch brothers, owners of Georgia-Pacific, the maker of all types of household paper products, pay the news media organizations to spread ugly stories about African Americans. These stories create among many whites a fear that is, for the most part, unwarranted but that causes some whites to react to African Americans in an unhealthy, and in the case of some police officers, deadly manner.

Our school system, from the very early days, has taught us that the only good that has been done in the world was done by Hebrews, Greeks, Latins, and others, and that the blacks made no significant contributions to life in America or the world. In the coming chapters, I will put that myth to rest for good. Up until the late seventies, American schools taught kids that blacks were inferior, and black adults were forced to believe or behave as if they were inferior. There was no place to turn our anger if we wished to challenge our ugly social system but toward one another. As such, many lost the will to achieve and drifted into a life of entropy, hurting one another with alcohol, drugs, guns, and other violence. In short, we were living the life that too many plutocrats imagined, designed, and implemented with perfection.

An example of how our social system has failed black kids came from my daughter today. She was presenting at a predominately black Minneapolis high school and found that all the kids—every kid she met—had very low self-esteem. None spoke about going to major universities. Their focus was on community colleges. Folks, this is 2016, and our kids are still learning to look at themselves through an inferior lens. This must stop.

You have been engaged in a conflicted social system and a one-sided educational system—a system that says all men are created equal, with equal opportunity to build wealth and to be happy as Americans, just like the majority. At the same time, the system has convinced you that it was impossible to live "as the white man lives." This conflicted system has caused you much confusion and consternation, and you have rebelled in exactly the way that was constructed. You have become a reflection of what was required in order to keep you from sharing equally in the great wealth of our country. You have been demeaned in a systematic, successful effort to keep you off balance, so that you would not be viewed as being worthy of sharing America's wealth.

Both our social system and our education system taught you well how to complain about injustice, but they have omitted teaching you how to change the undesirable conditions about which you complain. You must learn how our social system and political system operate, so that you can develop constructive programs to change the future trajectory of your life. Protests alone are not the solution for future change. You must learn how our social and economic systems operate. Folks, most importantly you most vote.

You did not receive a quality education in our public school system. You were trained not to desire the same positions, professions, and careers that are available to the majority, but somehow you still dream that it could be. The plutocrats' great desire is for you to accept positions that they consider menial, because they must have laborers to produce their wealth, just as the plantation owners did with our ancestors. Now I have nothing against common labor and hard work, but you should not become happy with low-paying jobs that have no positive future. Just like the plutocrats, you must begin to think big. Remember that there would be no America as we know it today without the intellect, blood, sweat, and tears of your predecessors.

So I say to you: learn to look for success stories in your work; look for ways to invent create, or improve your work space, so that one day you might develop or identify the one process, program, or gadget that will change how we live and that will make you famous and independently wealthy. Learn to turn a lemon into lemonade. Fall in love with your brothers, and support them in positive ways. Sacrifice for their well-being and share your knowledge openly. I call on educated African Americans: please do not forget your delinquent brothers, do not write them off, and do not move on until you have helped your brother to move on and upward as well.

THE FOUNDING FATHERS' PERSPECTIVE

Because the Founding Fathers of America were all white men, some white males continue to believe that the Constitution was written for them only. Frankly, that very well may have been the intent, but it most certainly is not explicitly stated in any documents anymore.

History teaches us that, in fact, if not for two states—South Carolina and Georgia—African Americans would have been included in both the

Declaration of Independence and the Constitution. Jefferson drafted a section of the Declaration of Independence that described slavery as against the "most sacred rights of life and liberty." Delegates from South Carolina and Georgia refused to sign the document, and some delegates from New England refused as well. So understand that, even as far back as 1776, most white men believed that all people should have equal rights.

However, just as our great country succumbs to the will of the few who are the loudest today, and the few who are the wealthiest, so did the Second Continental Congress in 1776. As such, blacks and women were labeled as less than, and some, both white and black, continue to believe that myth even today.

Now, some will read this and see it as a dislike for white Americans, but that would be a misrepresentation of my perspective. I am simply arguing that black boys, early in life, have been led to believe that they have or would have access to the best that America has to offer in education, wealth, business, and life in general, but at every turn in their lives, including in high school, they have been denied, and I don't think anyone can argue that point. What's worse is that they are blamed for being turned away at every door. What's even more destructive to the mental and physical health of our black boys is that they have lost faith in a social and legal system that has consistently turned its back on them for more than two hundred years.

Understanding Our Founding Documents

To understand our social system and the socialization process of African Americans, one must first embrace and understand our Constitution. I encourage you to read and reread our Constitution and to download a copy to your phone or other gadget for easy reference. Understanding our Constitution will give you the confidence to live the life that is promised you, not by those who hate, but by our Founding Fathers. Yes, I said *our* Founding Fathers, because in the original draft of the Declaration of Independence, you were included by Thomas Jefferson. You must start with the Declaration of Independence. The original draft that Jefferson submitted had some of the following included that were either deleted or altered.

And for the support of this declaration we mutually pledge to each other our lives, our fortunes, and our sacred honor.

In the below draft, note where Congress struck out some of the text written by Jefferson. It is, to a significant degree, contradictory and hypercritical to speak about Indians as "Savages" when the white men were taking the homeland of the Indian without any mercy or compassion. Also, note as you read the document that one of the primary concerns of the British is the violation of a most sacred right by placing some of their brethren—the Indian—into slavery. One would think that after living similar events at the hands of the British, locking a free people into slavery, the killing of Indians would have been unthinkable—especially since as history has shown that most Indian tribes wanted to be friendly to the point of teaching young America how to feed itself. The redacted document states:

> He has «excited domestic Insurrections amongst us, & has» endeavored to bring on the Inhabitants of our Frontiers, the merciless Indian Savages, whose known Rule of Warfare, is an undistinguished Destruction, of all Ages, Sexes, & Conditions ~~of existence. He has incited treasonable insurrections of our fellow-citizens, with the allurements of forfeiture & confiscation of our property. He has waged cruel war against human nature itself, violating it's most sacred rights of life and liberty in the persons of a distant people who never offended him, captivating & carrying them into slavery in another hemisphere, or to incur miserable death in their transportation thither. This piratical warfare, the opprobrium of INFIDEL powers, is the warfare of the CHRISTIAN king of Great Britain. Determined to keep open a market where MEN should be bought & sold, he has prostituted his negative for suppressing every legislative attempt to prohibit or to restrain this execrable commerce. And that this assemblage of horrors might want no fact of distinguished die, he is now exciting those very people to rise in arms among us, and to purchase that liberty of which he has deprived them, by murdering the people on whom he also~~

~~obtruded them. thus paying off former crimes committed against the LIBERTIES of one people, with crimes which he urges them to commit against the LIVES of another.~~ In every stage of these Oppressions we have Petitioned for Redress in the humblest Terms: Our repeated Petitions have been answered only by repeated Injury. A Prince whose Character is thus marked by every act which may define a Tyrant, is unfit to be the Ruler of a «free» People ~~who mean to be free. Future ages will scarcely believe that the hardiness of one man adventured, within the short compass of twelve years only, to lay a foundation so broad & so undisguised for tyranny over a people fostered & fixed in principles of freedom.~~

The Declaration of Independence

IN CONGRESS, JULY 4, 1776

The unanimous Declaration of the thirteen United States of America

When in the Course of human events it becomes necessary for one people to dissolve the political bands which have connected them with another, and to assume among the powers of the earth, the separate and equal station to which the Laws of Nature and of Nature's God entitle them, a decent respect to the opinions of mankind requires that they should declare the causes which impel them to the separation.

 We hold these truths to be self-evident, that all men are created equal, that they are endowed by their Creator with certain unalienable Rights, that among these are Life, Liberty and the pursuit of Happiness.—That to secure these rights, Governments are instituted among Men, deriving their just powers from the consent of the governed,—That whenever any Form of Government becomes destructive of these ends, it is the Right of the People to alter or to abolish it, and to institute new Government, laying its foundation on such principles and organizing its powers in such form, as to them shall seem most likely to affect their Safety and Happiness. Prudence, indeed, will dictate that Governments long established should not be changed for light and transient causes; and accordingly, all experience hath shewn, that mankind are more disposed to suffer, while evils are sufferable, than to right themselves by abolishing the forms to which they are accustomed. But when a long train of abuses and usurpations, pursuing invariably the same Object evinces a design to reduce them under absolute Despotism, it is their right, it is their duty, to throw off such Government, and to provide new Guards for their future security.— Such has been the patient sufferance of these Colonies; and such is now the necessity which constrains them to alter their former Systems of Government. The history of the present King of Great Britain is a history of repeated injuries and usurpations, all having in direct object the establishment of an absolute Tyranny over these States. To prove this, let Facts be submitted to a candid world.

He has refused his Assent to Laws, the most wholesome and necessary for the public good.

He has forbidden his Governors to pass Laws of immediate and pressing importance, unless suspended in their operation till his Assent should be obtained; and when so suspended, he has utterly neglected to attend to them.

He has refused to pass other Laws for the accommodation of large districts of people, unless those people would relinquish the right of Representation in the Legislature, a right inestimable to them and formidable to tyrants only.

He has called together legislative bodies at places unusual, uncomfortable, and distant from the depository of their public Records, for the sole purpose of fatiguing them into compliance with his measures.

He has dissolved Representative Houses repeatedly, for opposing with manly firmness his invasions on the rights of the people.

He has refused for a long time, after such dissolutions, to cause others to be elected; whereby the Legislative Powers, incapable of

Annihilation, have returned to the People at large for their exercise; the State remaining in the meantime exposed to all the dangers of invasion from without, and convulsions within.

He has endeavored to prevent the population of these States; for that purpose obstructing the Laws for Naturalization of Foreigners; refusing to pass others to encourage their migrations hither, and raising the conditions of new Appropriations of Lands.

He has obstructed the Administration of Justice by refusing his Assent to Laws for establishing Judiciary Powers.

He has made Judges dependent on his Will alone for the tenure of their offices, and the amount and payment of their salaries.

He has erected a multitude of New Offices, and sent hither swarms of Officers to harass our people and eat out their substance.

He has kept among us, in times of peace, Standing Armies without the Consent of our legislatures.

He has affected to render the Military independent of and superior to the Civil Power.

He has combined with others to subject us to a jurisdiction foreign to our constitution, and unacknowledged by our laws; giving his Assent to their Acts of pretended Legislation:

For quartering large bodies of armed troops among us:

For protecting them, by a mock Trial from punishment for any Murders which they should commit on the Inhabitants of these States:

For cutting off our Trade with all parts of the world:

For imposing Taxes on us without our Consent:

For depriving us in many cases, of the benefit of Trial by Jury:

For transporting us beyond Seas to be tried for pretended offences:

For abolishing the free System of English Laws in a neighboring Province, establishing therein an Arbitrary government, and enlarging its Boundaries so as to render it at once an example and fit instrument for introducing the same absolute rule into these Colonies:

For taking away our Charters, abolishing our most valuable Laws and altering fundamentally the Forms of our Governments:

For suspending our own Legislatures, and declaring themselves invested with power to legislate for us in all cases whatsoever.

He has abdicated Government here, by declaring us out of his Protection and waging War against us.

He has plundered our seas, ravaged our coasts, burnt our towns, and destroyed the lives of our people.

He is at this time transporting large Armies of foreign Mercenaries to compleat the works of death, desolation, and tyranny, already begun with circumstances of Cruelty & perfidy scarcely paralleled in the most barbarous ages, and totally unworthy the Head of a civilized nation.

He has constrained our fellow Citizens taken Captive on the high Seas to bear Arms against their Country, to become the executioners of their friends and Brethren, or to fall themselves by their Hands.

He has excited domestic insurrections amongst us, and has endeavored to bring on the inhabitants of our frontiers, the merciless Indian Savages whose known rule of warfare, is an undistinguished destruction of all ages, sexes and conditions.

In every stage of these Oppressions We Have Petitioned for Redress in the most humble terms: Our repeated Petitions have been answered only by repeated injury. A Prince, whose character is thus marked by every act which may define a Tyrant, is unfit to be the ruler of a free people.

Nor have We been wanting in attentions to our British brethren. We have warned them from time to time of attempts by their legislature to extend an unwarrantable jurisdiction over us. We have reminded them of the circumstances of our emigration and settlement here. We have appealed to their native justice and magnanimity, and we have conjured them by the ties of our common kindred to disavow these usurpations, which would inevitably interrupt our connections and correspondence. They too have been deaf to the voice of justice and of consanguinity. We must, therefore, acquiesce in the necessity, which denounces our Separation, and hold them, as we hold the rest of mankind, Enemies in War, in Peace Friends.

We, therefore, the Representatives of the United States of America, in General Congress, Assembled, appealing to the Supreme Judge of the world for the rectitude of our intentions, do, in the Name, and by Authority of the good People of these Colonies, solemnly publish and declare, That these United Colonies are, and of Right ought to be Free and Independent States; that they are Absolved from all Allegiance to the British Crown, and that all political connection between them and the State of Great Britain, is and ought to be totally dissolved; and that as Free and Independent States, they have full Power to levy War, conclude Peace, contract Alliances, establish Commerce, and to do all other Acts and Things which Independent States may of right do. And for the support of this Declaration, with a firm reliance on the protection of divine Providence, we mutually pledge to each other our Lives, our Fortunes, and our sacred Honor.

New Hampshire:
Josiah Bartlett, William Whipple, Matthew Thornton

Massachusetts:
John Hancock, Samuel Adams, John Adams, Robert Treat Paine, Elbridge Gerry

Rhode Island:
Stephen Hopkins, William Ellery

Connecticut:
Roger Sherman, Samuel Huntington, William Williams, Oliver Wolcott

New York:
William Floyd, Philip Livingston, Francis Lewis, Lewis Morris

New Jersey:
Richard Stockton, John Witherspoon, Francis Hopkinson, John Hart, Abraham Clark

Pennsylvania:
Robert Morris, Benjamin Rush, Benjamin Franklin, John Morton, George Clymer, James Smith, George Taylor, James Wilson, George Ross

Delaware:
Caesar Rodney, George Read, Thomas McKean

Maryland:
Samuel Chase, William Paca, Thomas Stone, Charles Carroll of Carrollton

Virginia:
George Wythe, Richard Henry Lee, Thomas Jefferson, Benjamin Harrison, Thomas Nelson, Jr., Francis Lightfoot Lee, Carter Braxton

North Carolina:
William Hooper, Joseph Hewes, John Penn

South Carolina:
Edward Rutledge, Thomas Heyward, Jr., Thomas Lynch, Jr., Arthur Middleton

Georgia:
Button Gwinnett, Lyman Hall, George Walton

Please note that when I say "white man," it is not inclusive of all white men, because obviously, without the help of some moral and ethical white men, blacks would have been completely destroyed during slavery and the Jim Crow era. As you read the Declaration of Independence, it is easy to capture the essence of the mental conflict in the document. On the one hand, demanding their human rights be respected, and on the other hand, doing whatever was necessary to protect what they perceived to be their natural rights—and oftentimes the two were very much at odds. In fact, some white males had created a utilitarian system that bent toward that which was good for them, and everyone else be damned—including, sometimes, white females.

THE US CONSTITUTION

Reading and understanding the Declaration of Independence is important; however, educating oneself on the Constitution is much more important. One of the things that most Middle Easterners, Chinese, Japanese, and others do prior to coming to America is to study our Constitution. In fact, they are more knowledgeable about our Constitution than the majority of our congressional leaders. They also study our financial system, including our financial laws, so that when they arrive, they are prepared for success. They have a clear understanding of the desires of the wealthy plutocrats, and they come to America to start businesses that meet those needs.

Yes, I understand that many African Americans rebelled because they were denied opportunities to excel in too many American organizations. I agree that we should have the same opportunity, but if those opportunities are based on disingenuous promises and we have been misled, what must one do?

What we should do is seek out the desires of the wealthy and fulfill those desires, just as many Latinos, Chinese, Japanese, and Middle Easterners have done with great skill. They have carved out essential businesses in neighborhoods all over America, which is making them an invaluable part of the communities in which they live. But we were so bamboozled during our socialization process that we could not open our eyes to see the potential for turning a lemon into sweet lemonade.

The Constitution is the most important document that we have in America. I will review the sections that I believe are most important to you as African Americans, but please read the complete document so that you gain the knowledge and deep understanding of the documents that govern our social system. Your knowledge of the Constitution should far exceed that of those who were not born here in America—such as many of our friends from

Mexico, China, Japan, and the Middle East. If you wonder why our friends from other countries appear to be more successful in our social system than you are, it is because they have not been bamboozled by our social system, and they understand it better than most Americans because they have become scholars of our social system and our capitalistic system.

It is important that you read and find understanding and meaning in the Constitution, but the amendments are also important, and here I will share and discuss several of these with you.

Preamble

We the People of the United States, in Order to form a more perfect Union, establish Justice, insure domestic Tranquility, provide for the common defense, promote the general Welfare, and secure the Blessings of Liberty to ourselves and our Posterity, do ordain and establish this Constitution for the United States of America.

We start with the Thirteenth Amendment, which was ratified on December 6, 1865:

Section 1. Neither slavery nor involuntary servitude, except as a punishment for crime whereof the party shall have been duly convicted, shall exist within the United States, or any place subject to their jurisdiction.

In fact, Lincoln had long ago determined that slavery was inhumane. Watching the brutal treatment of slaves when traveling the Mississippi River as a young man instilled memories in his mind that he could never dismiss. So, as the Civil War was escalating, he considered, among other things, the use of slaves to help fight the war. Thus, in "September 1862, following the Union victory at the Battle of Antietam in Maryland, Lincoln issued the Emancipation Proclamation, declaring that all slaves in territory still in rebellion on January 1, 1863, would be declared forever free."

The freed slaves proved to be a magnificent fighting force that helped to turn the war in favor of the North for good. If you research your ancestors, you will find that many of them were heroes in this battle for our freedom.

> **Section 2.** Congress shall have power to enforce this article by appropriate legislation.

Brothers, stop behaving like slaves and enslaving your brothers and sisters in drugs, alcohol, and other behaviors that serve to limit their ability to grow and reach their full, God-given intellectual talents. Start today sharing your knowledge and love for one another...let's demonstrate to the world that we are in control of our destiny and we are not slaves to any people.

Next is the Fifteenth Amendment, and it is most important.

> **Section 1.** The right of citizens of the United States to vote shall not be denied or abridged by the United States or by any State on account of race, color, or previous condition of servitude.
>
> **Section 2.** The Congress shall have power to enforce this article by appropriate legislation.

As you know, in recent years, particularly since President Obama has been in office, some states have worked hard to deny black Americans their right to vote, and that is simply not acceptable. My fellow Americans, the only way to change our social system and democracy for the long term is to vote. Yes, picketing and marching can help after the fact, but please understand that your vote can prevent police brutality, courtroom biases by judges, and laws that serve to limit your growth potential. Next, please understand this, and it is very important. In fact, I will write about this in detail later. There will come a time in the future when you will be the most powerful voting bloc in America. Please do yourself, your family, and America a favor, and vote.

The Twenty-Fourth Amendment was ratified on January 23, 1964, but several states did not abide by the law until the Supreme Court ruled in a six-to-three decision in 1966 that a poll tax for any voting was unconstitutional. Consider this important fact, please. As African Americans, we were granted the freedom to vote in some states only in 1966. Even today some African Americans are subjected to inferior education, but we are expected to compete at the same level as others who have had the right to a quality education for three hundred years. Frankly, I would argue that, based on the restricted educational opportunities African Americans have had to navigate, they have surprised many with their rapid intellectual growth in an environment that has been hostile toward them. Similarly, it is vital that African Americans take full opportunity of their right to vote and demonstrate to the country how seriously they take this responsibility.

Section 1. The right of citizens of the United States to vote in any primary or other election for President or Vice President, for electors for President or Vice President, or for Senator or Representative in Congress, shall not be denied or abridged by the United States or any state by reason of failure to pay any poll tax or other tax.

Section 2. The Congress shall have power to enforce this article by appropriate legislation.

It is time that you exercise your right to vote in every election. Believe me, you could change police brutality and the employment situation of your community if you would only exercise your right to vote in every election. In the coming years, you will have the opportunity to control the outcome of every general election, but you must start preparing now by voting.

When I think about all the black teens and kids who are killed by the police, tears come to my eyes. However, what I weep about most is that too many African Americans do not vote. In fact, as many as 37 percent of African American citizens who were eligible to vote in the 2012 election did not exercise that most important right in our democracy.

You have come to believe that your vote does not matter, and that could not be farther from the truth. Consider the fact that the city of Ferguson, Missouri, is at least 67 percent African American, and only three of the police officers were black when Michael Brown was shot to death in the middle of the street. I recall all the protests and marching in the city and even some disorderly conduct, which is never acceptable. I recall wanting very much to join the marchers. I also recall thinking that protesting has proven to work in years past, and it was possible that protests could work now.

However, upon deeper reflection, I could not help but ask myself why my brothers do not vote…in places like Ferguson, Chicago, Memphis, Atlanta, Houston, and many other cities and counties where you can control who leads your cities. Far too often you choose to allow white men, some of whom are great supporters and some, I am sure, who are racists, to decide your fate and to lead your cities because you simply do not vote for your future and the future of your kids. That, in and of itself, is the bigger tragedy, and it is simply not acceptable.

Just consider, if African Americans had voted in the city of Ferguson and possibly changed the dynamics of their city, Michael Brown might be alive today. You have no choice. You most vote for the future of your family and other loved ones. If you do not vote, you have zero chance of changing the systematically socially constructed biased system that has caused you to lose faith in a system that the Founding Fathers said you have a right to enjoy. What's even worse, your acceptance is, in fact, a confirmation of a social system that has left you behind and caused you to lose faith in your ability to achieve the dreams that you desired when you set foot in the first grade of school.

Remember the joy and excitement that you had as you entered the first grade. Remember the great dreams that your mom sent with you as you stepped into that classroom in the first grade…and so you must get busy saving the future for others, so that they do not lose their dreams, as far too many have done.

Research has shown that African American boys are extremely creative and bright as they enter the first grade. However, because you were not allowed to display your creativity and you were forced to follow rules that limited your ability to create and to be yourself, you quickly became someone that you were not familiar with—someone whose intellectual development was limited, someone who was eventually labeled as not being very bright—and far too often you were placed in special classes that only served to cause you to lose confidence in yourself and in the future that you had dreamed of, causing far too many of you to check out of a biased social system that simply did not help you grow intellectually, a system designed to reward similarity and conformity, not creativity and intellect.

Lesson 7: Your Great History

Before you can move forward to become your greatest, you must understand your history, a history that helped to shape this great country, a history that has demonstrated your bravery and love for God and America. Only by having a clear picture firmly planted in your mind of the positive past can you reshape the future. One reason some elite white males are willing to defend what they believe to be their true rights is that history has taught them to believe them true—too many historical stories have lifted them up and degraded you.

It is time that you learned all the great, positive things about your history, so that you can retell true and positive stories about your history. You must plant your beliefs in your true history, not the history that has been constructed to cause you to hate society and to mistreat your brothers—not a history that has misled you into degradation, but one that lifts up you, your family, and your communities. Your true history is one of love, family, support, and creativity. In the coming chapters, I will get you started on that positive historical journey.

So, you must read and reread our Constitution, so that you can take full advantage of its meaning. You have believed what you were taught, and when those teachings were shown to be false, you decided to reject the system in totality. Understand that you were bamboozled in our poor educational system, but it is time that you learn how our capitalistic system works and start to benefit from our progressive system, just as Latinos, Asians, and others have.

But first, I repeat, you must exercise your Thirteenth Amendment right and vote. Folks, you will not change your future if you do not vote.

> Be as proud of your race today as our fathers were in days of yore. We have beautiful history, and we shall create another in the future that will astonish the world.
>
> —MARCUS GARVEY, *THE PHILOSOPHY AND OPINIONS OF MARCUS GARVEY*

CHAPTER 8

Why Police Are Killing Black Kids

MISGUIDED AMERICANS

THERE ARE MANY REASONS POLICE are killing black kids, and in this chapter, I discuss this issue from three different perspectives. First, I offer a brief historical perspective—the real reasons for the divide among the races. Second, I offer some very scary and factual reasons, and finally, this will not be popular, but I offer a strong theoretical argument in defense of some overly aggressive police actions. To really understand how we got to this point of great divide and mistrust for one another, one must understand this problem from a historical perspective.

To comprehend the full context of African Americans, one should start with the great history of the forgotten black popes, the Black Madonna, and Mansu Musa and the empire of Mali. However, each of those stories alone would fill a three-hundred-page book. To tell the story so that it fits within the context of this book, I will start with a brief overview of slavery.

Many historians believe that the greatest travesty of American history and the world was the transatlantic slave trade. It is estimated that between 1.2 million and four million slaves died while en route to the New World. Further, it is believed that more than ten million Africans died during four centuries of the Atlantic slave trade. However, when one considers the number of documented trips from Africa to the New World, those numbers would appear to be inaccurate. I believe that those numbers are but a small percentage of the actual African lives lost during the slave trade. There are no exact numbers regarding how many slaves died during slavery, but some scientists believe that, due to the hard labor and diseases contracted in the New World, at least 50 percent died; in other words, half of the African American population likely died.

Consider that in 1860 the African American population was approximately four million. One might ask a simple question: Was half the population already decimated because of the inhumane treatment they had received? We will never really know because of the poorly maintained records during the slavery period. I am hopeful that scholars will continue to research this awful period in American and world history in an effort to correct our history, so that the healing of America can move toward completion. I believe that as long as the truth is hidden from African Americans regarding slavery and the facts of slavery are not accepted by whites, we will continue to live in a divided America that is restrictive to our future because we simply devote too much time to this complicated and complex historical event. Yes, in a great sense, our bodies live in the future, but our spirits and our minds are stuck in the past because of our fear of learning the true story of this horrible period in our history.

The FBI's Report

On October 17, 2006, the FBI unclassified a portion of a sensitive law enforcement report titled "White Supremacist Infiltration of Law Enforcement." That report offered some startling and scary news. Here are some actual excerpts from the report:

> This intelligence assessment provides an overview of White supremacist infiltration of law enforcement and derives its information from FBI investigations and open sources available as of August 2006.
>
> The primary threat from infiltration or recruitment arises from the areas of intelligence collection and exploitation, which can lead to investigative breaches and can jeopardize the safety of law enforcement sources and personnel.

White supremacist presence among law enforcement personnel is a concern due to the access they may possess to restricted areas vulnerable to sabotage and to elected officials or protected persons, whom they could see as potential targets for violence.

The intelligence acquired through the successful infiltration of law enforcement by one White supremacist group can benefit other groups due to the multiple allegiances White supremacists typically hold.

This assessment examines White supremacist infiltration of law enforcement from perspectives of both strategic infiltrations by organized groups and self-initiated infiltration by law enforcement persons sympathetic to White supremacist causes. The primary threat from infiltration or recruitment arises from the area of intelligence collection and exploitation, which can lead to investigative breaches and can jeopardize the safety of law enforcement sources or personnel.

White supremacist leaders and groups have historically shown an interest in infiltrating law enforcement communities or recruiting law enforcement personnel.

Since coming to law enforcement attention in late 2004, the term "ghost skins" has gained currency among White supremacists to describe those who avoid overt display of their beliefs to blend into society and covertly advance White supremacist causes. One internet posting describes this effort as a form of role-playing in which "to create the character, you must get inside the mind of the person you are trying to duplicate." Such role-playing has application to ad-hoc and organized law enforcement infiltration. At least one White supremacist group has reportedly encouraged ghost skins to seek positions in law enforcement for the capability of alerting skinhead crews of pending investigative action against them.

Thus, it should be, and it is, fairly easy to identify some of the causes for so much police violence toward African American males, and to a similar degree and concern, African American women. The FBI's research clearly indicates that many of our police departments are corrupted by radical white supremacist groups, including members of the KKK.

Recently while in Phoenix, I learned that local police request to ride along with Arizona State University students in an effort to recruit them into their supremacist network. That is sickening. I can't help but wonder if that is a method employed around the country by police departments. One must ask the question: Are African Americans being killed because these groups are in control of many of our police departments?

The next question that we must engage and acknowledge is whether President Clinton knew that his "three strikes crime bill" would primarily affect African American males. The answer must be yes; however, I do not believe that he understood the long-term ramifications of such a disastrous decision. He could not have known that police around the country would use the law to unlawfully frame African American men. However, consider that Bill Clinton studied at Oxford University and completed his law degree at Yale; given that background, one must conclude that his intellect was such that he understood exactly what he was doing. Was he speaking good things about African Americans and at the same time selling us out? Because of the law that he proposed, one in three African American males has a criminal record; therefore, they cannot exercise their right to vote in most states. He was very proud of this law, as this quote clearly indicates:

> JACKSON HOLE, Wyo.—President Clinton on Saturday hailed the life prison sentence given to the first man convicted under the federal government's "three strikes" law and prodded Congress to approve his languishing anti-terrorism bill.

Was Clinton a friend of African Americans? Or was he used by the Republicans as the lead in their effort to diminish the little power that blacks had…voting power? With this law in place, police were empowered to lock up as many African American males as possible, and did they ever. Was this the first step in the Republicans' bid to control the House, Senate, and eventually White House?

Though the police had been aggressive when it came to addressing African American males for years, now this single law offered them the power to be even more aggressive when they addressed African American males. So, too, this law offered our social system the opportunity to continue, and in fact, reinforce, negative stereotypes of African American males by portraying them as drug dealers, drug addicts, and bad people who must be put in their place. One was hard pressed to turn on the news and not see African American males in handcuffs being charged with all sorts of crimes. In fact, for many years, white crime was either not televised, or it was given a very brief review before the subject was changed to the very bad African Americans, so that the media could maximize sells to white America. African Americans have been used in many ways to grow and maximize capital, but this form of capitalism has damaged all Americans' psyches, possibly to the point of no return.

This horrible portrayal of African American males in the media continued a history of shaping and encouraging negative and oftentimes harmful beliefs among many whites. This relentless media attack on some African Americans was purposely fed to the American public in such a way that it appeared that all African Americans were complicit in the horrible acts that drugs brought to too many communities. This messaging from the media had a particularly destructive influence among uneducated whites, because they tend to believe the media explicitly without asking critical questions or performing any research of their own volition. They could not, and would not, ask this simple question: Can forty million people be that bad?

It does not take the brightest person in the room to answer that question with a categorical no. The truth is that this type of criminal behavior was isolated to a very few African American males in a few cities, but all were suddenly a target because of this new discriminatory law. All of them became suspects in the eyes of Bill Clinton's law.

The very worst part of these misguided reports by the media was that African Americans watched this on TV and listened to the news on the radio, and many came to believe these lies themselves, including yours truly. Much of this propaganda was created and generated because of Clinton's three-strikes law, which proved to be disastrous for all African American males, not just the real criminals. The irony of this misguided law was that many African Americans actually bought into this exaggerated myth that we were bad people, and so they determined to live down to those lies.

Why Some Police Shoot First

This leads me into my doctoral research discussion regarding why some police appear to be overly aggressive when they encounter African American males, even if they are not racist and do not have biased tendencies. Simply stated, many police were bamboozled into believing that what they were doing was based on the law, and to some degree they were correct. Because of the three-strikes law and the relentless media coverage of any, and it seemed every, African American coming close to violating the law, many police came to believe in a real sense that all African American males were nefarious or predisposed to crime when that is the furthest thing from the truth. Many whites embraced this false belief and did so even today because of the news and because they have never engaged an African American in a conversation of any kind.

It was refreshing to see Paul Ryan recently state that his view of poor people was wrong. For the House leader to say that confirmed that the images he held of African Americans were composed by our social system and the media, which is funded by wealthy white men who control large companies. If a staunch conservative can admit that he was wrong, it is indeed a step in the right direction.

My research identified the primary reasons why we hold strong beliefs and often act on these beliefs, even when they are proved to be false. My research identified the three major heuristics that we access when we make decisions. These heuristics are activated intuitively. They are important to understand, so I will review them briefly.

Even Aristotle understood that human reasoning was flawed. He found that an individual's experience was of great value when it came to complex reasoning. Though he did not use the word "heuristics," that is exactly what he identified.

In 1972, two scientists, Newel and Simon, were responsible for the name "heuristics" gaining broad attention when they used the term to describe an effortless process that replaced complex algorithms. Simon, the father of heuristics research in judgment and decision making, argued that "because people lack the capacity to compute large amounts of information, they find ways to arrive at satisfactory solutions." Simon went on to simplify his definition by insisting that humans simply do not have the capacity to think through complex decisions, and so they take shortcuts. Most of the time, their decisions are correct, but occasionally they lead to systematically biased decisions because humans rely on experience.

However, Simon did not identify the specific heuristics humans use or apply when they take shortcuts during their decision-making process, and for the first time, my research identified the heuristics that we access during our decision-making process. In fact, my research found that humans not only take shortcuts, but they often apply a "rule of thumb seeking a satisfactory solution using heuristics." My research also found that reliance on heuristics generally leads to satisfactory solutions, but reliance on heuristics can also cause predictable and systematic errors that lead to disastrous results—like the killing of African American kids when under extreme pressure. When under extreme pressure, the brain simply cannot judge the difference between what's real or not real, and so it will access one of three heuristics when making immediate decisions.

My research identified ten heuristics that humans can access when making decisions, but under pressure or when the decision is urgent and has critical consequences, humans generally access three heuristics intuitively or naturalistically, not rationally. These three heuristics are shaped by our everyday experiences, which include the media, our social structure, friends, family, church, school, and of course, our environment, and so on. The vast majority of our police are white, so I ask you: Where and how are their experiences shaped?

The three heuristics that humans access when they are under pressure are as follows:

- availability—perceived frequencies of events are affected and subjected probability (Kahneman et al. 1982, 164).

- representative—the tendency to view a sample drawn from a population as highly representative of that population (Kahneman et al. 1982)
- confirmation—the human inclination to see what we expect to see from our environment (Rehak et al. 2010)

Now consider, if the police who killed so many African American males had a bad or negative experience with African Americans, or grew up in an environment that taught them to distrust and dislike African Americans, or watched Fox News and viewed an ugly incident that showed African American men causing harm to others or doing something illegal, how might they react under pressure when accessing these heuristics intuitively? What would they see, believe, and feel during an actual event when they had to make a split-second decision? How would the brain process the input regarding what they were viewing as a dangerous and urgent situation?

Here is exactly how the brain will process what they are experiencing as an event unfolds during what they perceive as a dangerous and urgent situation. First, the officers will access a heuristic in the brain that is representative of what they believe they are seeing. This will be the most available, and in most cases, the most recent, event or experience or the most profound event in their life. Suppose they just finished watching Fox News and saw an African American with a gun or in a threatening situation. During what the brain perceives as an actual emergency, it will quickly attempt to confirm that the information being received is representative of what the person is experiencing in real time, and the individual will react based on the perception of the situation. Under extreme pressure, the human brain simply does not have the cognitive capacity to analyze circumstances in detail; instead, it will access the most available and representative information or knowledge and seek quick confirmation. Again, once the information is confirmed as a real event based on the most representative and available information, the individual will respond because the event has been validated as real in real time.

This might explain why, in some cases, police officers are in disbelief themselves after a horrible and inexcusable event of taking a life. This does not excuse those police who are indeed part of racist or supremacist groups, as we identified previously, but it can help us to explain why some good cops can make systematically flawed decisions that are biased and could have life-and-death results.

I am challenging social scientists to examine the background of those officers and to compare similarities in background and lifestyles. For example, I think research will reveal that they are similar in the news they watch, the churches they attend, the segregated communities they live in, the lack of minority friends, the type of high school they attended, and the type of friends they engage with. I am convinced that this type of research will reveal that our socialization process is in need of overhauling at its very core for all Americans.

How to Change Their Cognitive Triggers

When I was working on my undergraduate degree at DePaul University in Chicago, I decided to analyze churches across the city for my capstone class. I wanted to understand how we, as Americans, could expect workplace diversity to be successful when our nearly five hundred thousand churches are segregated. I wanted to learn if it were practical to even consider workplace diversity when our religion has divided us in so many ways—particularly along racial lines. Although I did not answer my core thesis regarding how we as a society could expect synergy regarding workplace diversity because of our segregated churches, I did confirm that 99 percent of the churches I visited were segregated. That is a social problem for our country now, and possibly forever, unless we as humans place us first. So as challenging as this is to say, I believe that our religious systems must be rebuilt to become totally inclusive. I believe Lakewood Church in Houston, Texas, can offer us a beginning model to consider. Yes, this is a challenge, but certainly possible—just as all things are possible in God's eyes.

Based on this single complicated challenge, I wondered if it's even possible that we can ever expect our social system to operate as a dynamic one. I would propose that we can start with our media. As I write this book, I find myself watching the NCAA basketball playoffs, and I believe that there are no better sports, period, anywhere. Now as a social scientist, I tend to notice social situations in all of their complexities. While watching the women's NCAA playoffs, I could not help but notice that in almost every game, the lead announcer was a male, and most often a white male, and the commentators were female. I also noted that the commentators seemed to be much better in terms of speaking and knowledge about the game, but for some reason, they were not the lead announcers.

This, to me, is simply crazy. I can only surmise that these guys are full-time employees, and so the leadership felt compelled to have them lead the sports broadcast, or, just as in previous years, it was important for the leadership to ensure that those whom they considered to be their equals had work, so they might have the capacity to feed their families no matter their qualifications and no matter whether others had the same opportunity to feed their families or not.

My point here is the media has to start to challenge this craziness and fulfill their responsibility in our social system. So, too, we, as Americans, must begin to challenge such situations. What makes this particular situation even worse is the fact that women make up 51 percent of our population and white males are only approximately 37 percent. If those who are Latino but claim to be white are removed from the white male population, the percentage drops to about 30 percent in 2015. However, according to the US Census, the white male population will drop to 22.5 percent in 2050 when the Latinos who identify themselves as white are removed from the number.

Next, we must rewrite American history and tell the stories of all the people who helped make America great. For example, white Americans might have died of hunger had the Indians decided not to teach them how to feed themselves. So, too, much of America's wealth and architecture would not have been possible without the sweat and tears of African Americans. In fact, the Civil War might have been lost if not for the brave fighting of African American soldiers. I encourage you to dig into your great history, a history that made America a superpower, and a history that will lift you up and teach you about your greatness, your intellect, your bravery, and your persistence.

I dedicate much of the next chapter to your history because our schools and colleges will not, for two reasons. First, the economics just don't work out for the publishers. When African Americans represent only about 12 to 15 percent of the population, those in power are not compelled to commit dollars and cents to research and tell their true story. Second, it's simply too painful to tell an American story that reveals the fact that millions of Africans died in this land, not en route from Africa, but here in America from hard labor, beatings, shootings, hangings, raping, and torture. If my ancestors were behind such mass killings, I'd probably wish to hide those historical facts also.

Finally, all current and potential police must be assessed regarding how stereotypes unconsciously influence their perception. We, as citizens, have a right to know the beliefs of those who are sworn to protect us. Harvard University, in collaboration with several other universities, created an excellent assessment tool that is now available that can assist leaders of police departments during the officer selection process. The assessment should not necessarily be used to screen individuals out but should be used to identify those officers who need some type of sensitivity training or support. You can locate the assessment at https://implicit.harvard.edu/implicit/takeatest.html.

LESSON 8: YOUR SOCIAL ORDER, OUR SOCIAL SYSTEM

Today is your day to start living the life that you were born to live, and the only way to start is to develop a deep and clear understanding of your history, African American history, a history that you will not learn in the American school system. If you have only one takeaway from this book, it should be a deep commitment to learning and sharing your history with your family and friends. Your history is a proud history, one that made America and the world what it is today. Simply stated, there could be no world, no America as we know it today, without both the brains and muscles of Africans, and thus African Americans.

Please do not simply Google "African American history." Go to the best libraries in your city and start researching African American history. Visit some of the libraries in Africa online. As you research African and African

American history, keep in mind that only the strong Africans survived the journey from Africa to the New World, and only the strongest of those survived the inhumane treatment here in America. All others perished. Thus, your bloodline is one of strength, perseverance, persistence, intellect, and love.

You are born of fame and talent. How else can one explain the great achievements of African Americans? Every time we are given the opportunity to compete in any arena, we compete well. However, there is one arena that has been denied African Americans for the most part, and that's the C-suite, where only 3 to 5 percent of the population are minority or female. However, in the coming years, you will have the opportunity to join the C-suite team because your creative and diverse intellect will be in great demand. Will you be ready?

Next, I beg of you to turn off the TV, particularly the news. A big part of your socialization process takes place over the airways. While the process is subtle, it affects you at a deep cognitive level. Its primary purpose has been, and continues to be to a great degree, to systematically demean your intellect and talent. Far too often, the media is controlled by large organizations only concerned with selling products to the majority, and it does not matter whether they are liberal or conservative or as mainstream as CNN; they will portray you as the demon of our American society because that type of news attracts capital. Portraying the majority in such a light would surely diminish their capital income quickly. Don't watch the news.

Please remember that the media is funded by corporate America, and corporate America is run primarily by the wealthy—some of whom are indeed racist, but all are in it for the capital. Thus, watching the news, and in most cases, any TV, is a mental waste of time for you, because the news and TV executives will search high and low to find any negative news that the majority of America will pay for, and the majority of America, yes, is white for now.

It is inevitable that you will walk away from any news broadcast upset because the reporters, in their quest to keep their jobs or be promoted, will cast any news regarding African Americans in a bad light. In fact, just recently one of the CBS executives said that "while Trump might be bad for America, he is very good for their bottom line." Now we all know that Trump is a racist and most likely harbors racists and extremists in his organization, just as many other Fortune 1000 companies do even today. So if a television executive embraces that behavior openly because of dollars and cents, what is he doing privately?

Finally, you must gain a more in-depth understanding of how our social system and capitalist system is affecting you at a deep cognitive level and a financial level as well. Know that capital drives everything in America, including religion and our divided churches. One method of growing and retaining wealth for the wealthy is to drive up productivity and to push wages down, and one way to drive down wages is to have the least of us fight for a few jobs—while in fact, there were many jobs for everyone here in America until the wealthy shipped jobs and work to China, Thailand, Vietnam, India, and other countries in an effort to drive down wages. They have forced too many of you to accept menial jobs that will not feed you and will most certainly not feed your family—and then blame you for not working. You must understand our capitalistic system is one that is conflicted and constructed to serve primarily those who have wealth or are connected or have privileges to which we do not have access. However, there is a greater wealth that we must embrace, and that's family.

> Of all the rocks upon which we build our lives, we are reminded today that family is the most important. And we are called to recognize and honor how critical every father is to that foundation. Fathers are teachers and coaches. They are mentors and role models. They are examples of success and the men who constantly push us toward it. But if we are honest with ourselves, we'll admit that too many fathers also are missing—missing from too many lives and too many homes. They have abandoned their responsibilities, acting like boys instead of men. And the foundations of our families are weaker because of it.
>
> —Barack Obama

CHAPTER 9

History of Inventions and Creations: Who Really Made America Great?

IT IS SHAMEFUL THAT OUR education system, and most writers, have left out the great accomplishments of African Americans and our brothers and sisters in Africa. For that reason, this chapter is dedicated to highlighting some of those great accomplishments.

When I was working on my PhD, I needed a break from academic research and writing, and so I took a much-deserved break and wrote a short book that told the stories of some of our greatest African American heroes, and that was fun. The book is titled *Sam the Sorcerer vs. American Heroes*. The idea for the book came from events regarding one of my best friends, Sam. One day while I was visiting Sam and his wife in the Phoenix area, Sam, just as he always does, began to argue and put his wife down. I said, "Sam, you are a mean man, and I am going to write a book about you. I think I'll name it *Sam the Sorcerer*." From there the idea evolved into me telling true stories about our African American heroes through the eyes of a fictitious character named Sam the Sorcerer. I will introduce you to some of those heroes and the great and rich history of African Americans. You will be amazed.

Benjamin Banneker was born free on November 9, 1731, in the British colony named Maryland. He was a brilliant scientist who predicted a solar eclipse in 1789, when two eminent white scientists had decreed that there would not be one. Banneker was correct, declaring that the other scientists' calculations were seriously flawed. Banneker went on to work on the design and survey for the capital city. He was so bright that when Major L'Enfant resigned as lead of the project for building the capitol and left with the documented plans, Banneker helped to reproduce them from memory. It can be argued that without Benjamin Banneker, there might be no capital city—or certainly not one that resembles the capital as we know it today. In fact, many believe that Banneker actually created the original drawings of the capital and that's why he could easily redraw them from memory.

Norbert Rillieux was born on a plantation in New Orleans on March 17, 1806—six years before Louisiana became a state. He was forbidden from attending the best schools in New Orleans; thus, his father, an affluent French immigrant, sent him off to Paris to study. Upon returning to New Orleans, he noted the danger slaves were in when they attempted to refine sugar by pouring hot crude sugar from barrel to barrel in an effort to create enough evaporation to start the refining process. He submitted a patent in 1926 describing how he would improve the steam engine so that it could become an evaporator. This was a big hit, and he continued to make improvements to the evaporator system. He also offered a method for dealing with the yellow fever epidemic in New Orleans by draining the swamps where mosquitoes lived, but city officials refused to use it initially because he was black, allowing thousands of people to die.

Benjamin Montgomery (1819–77) was born a slave in Loudon County, Virginia. In the late 1850s, he invented a more advanced propeller for river steamboats that navigated the waters around plantations. His invention was different and much better than those previously in use. Unlike other propellers, which pushed and forced the boats along the water, his propeller was constructed on the canoe paddling principle. Thus, the blades could cut through water from any angle with little resistance, so boats could move faster. He actually talked about testing his new invention with a steam engine, but he was unable to get a patent because of the Dred Scott decision in the Supreme Court…slaves could not apply for or receive patents.

Alexander Miles (1838–1918) invented the modern-day elevator design. Why is that important? Although Miles may not have invented the first elevator, his design was very important. Alexander Miles improved the method of the opening and closing of elevator doors, and he developed the closing of the elevator shaft when an elevator was not positioned at a floor. Miles created an automatic mechanism that closed access to the shaft. His patent is still used for most elevators today because they still work under the basic principle of automated opening and closing of doors. His life and his invention helped to break down racial barriers in many ways.

Elijah McCoy, born in 1843 or 1844 in Colchester, Ontario, Canada (there is no official record of birth), invented the self-lubricating cup that was originally used on trains so they did not have to stop to be lubricated. This invention was also used in automobiles and every other device that needed to be lubricated to operate continuously. In fact, this invention became so famous that the name "the real McCoy" was created.

Lewis Howard Latimer was born in 1848 in Chelsea, Massachusetts, and is the inventor of the Latimer lamp. However, more important and less known is that he was friends with Alexander Graham Bell. In 1876, Bell asked Latimer to share a drawing of the telephone that he had invented, and it is well known that when Bell applied for the telephone patent in 1876, it was Latimer's drawing that he presented.

Andrew Jackson Beard was born into slavery in 1849. He was uneducated but brilliant. He created and patented two separate plows and sold his ideas for a handsome sum. He went into the real estate business, buying and selling houses, and accumulated more wealth. He created and patented a coupling that could connect trains automatically, saving limbs and lives. He sold that invention for $50,000 to a firm in New York.

Jan Matzeliger (1852–89), who was from Suriname, invented a shoe-lasting machine. Why is that important? The shoe-lasting machine increased the availability of shoes and decreased the price of footwear. Matzeliger's shoe-lasting machine increased shoe production tremendously. The result was the employment of more unskilled workers and the proliferation of low-cost, high-quality footwear for people around the world.

Granville T. Woods, was born April 23, 1856, in Columbus, Ohio—a free man because the Northwest Ordinance of 1787 did not allow slavery in the territory from which Ohio became a state. He had over sixty patents, which included the telephone transmitter, called the telegraphy; rail telegraphy that helped trains to communicate and prevented many accidents; and the device that powered trains with electricity.

Garrett Augustus Morgan was born on March 4, 1877, to Sydney and Elizabeth Morgan. He was extremely disadvantaged, with few educational opportunities. He invented the gas mask, originally known as the safety hood. It saved not only the lives of firefighters and soldiers, but of welders worldwide. He also invented the first hair straightener in America; and he invented the electric light and sold the patent to GE for $40,000.

Thomas Jennings was born a free man in 1791 in New York City. He founded an early dry-cleaning process that restored clothes to a new appearance. He owned a large dry cleaning and clothing business in New York City and was the first black man in the United States to obtain a US patent.

Daniel Hale Williams, born on January 18, 1856, to Daniel and Sarah Williams, was a free person of free parents. He was the fifth of seven children and was constantly reminded about the importance of education. He performed the first successful open-heart surgery.

George Washington Carver was born a slave in 1864 in Diamond Grove, Missouri, during the Civil War. He and his mother were kidnapped from their plantation by raiders. His mother was never returned, but the slave owners paid a ransom for his return. Young George was accepted as a student at Highland University, but when he showed up, he was rejected and turned away because of the color of his skin. His persistence led him to study and eventually teach at Iowa State University. Booker T. Washington recruited Carver to teach at Tuskegee Normal and Industrial Institute. It was here that he taught the world how crop rotation could help make healthier vegetables. He also discovered that legumes, such as peanuts, were superior in nutrients and oils. This great finding helped him to produce peanut butter, shampoo, and coffee. In fact, he created over four hundred products from peanuts and sweet potatoes in one year.

Ernest Everett Just was born on August 14, 1883, in Charleston, South Carolina. Knowing that he could not obtain a quality education in South Carolina, his mother, a schoolteacher, urged him to go north to Kimball Union

Academy, located in New Hampshire. This high school was well known for preparing students for the rigor of excellent universities. He graduated at the top of his class, and thus he was acceptable at Dartmouth College, where he graduated again at the top of his class. Though he was exceptionally bright, he was refused jobs at predominantly white colleges. He was eventually offered a position at Howard University in Washington, DC, at a very low salary. He received a PhD from the University of Chicago in zoology after studying there for just one year. Dr. Just was one of the inventors of the microscope, which led to many discoveries thereafter and saved countless lives.

Henry Brown invented the modern-day fireproof safe, patented on November 2, 1886. This fire- and accident-proof safe was made of forged metal and required a key to open its lock.

Frederick McKinley Jones was born in 1893 in Cincinnati, Ohio, and he was orphaned when he was nine years old. Always intrigued by machines, he made it possible for food to be delivered across the country and the world with refrigeration, which was never considered previously. He invented the refrigeration design to operate on the top of trucks and in planes, so that food could be delivered worldwide and remain fresh. I guess one might say that without Frederick McKinley Jones and George Washington Carver, the peoples of the world might have starved. He also patented the first ticket-dispensing machine on September 25, 1928.

David Nelson Crosthwait Jr. was born in 1898 in Kansas City. He attended Purdue University after graduating with high honors from high school. He graduated with honors from Purdue and also completed his master of science degree in mechanical engineering. Crosthwait worked for CA Dunham Company, located in Michigan City, Indiana. There he patented more than fifty inventions. He was most proud of a gigantic heating system he designed for the Radio City Music Hall in New York City.

Percy Lavon Julian was born in 1899 in Montgomery, Alabama, to a very poor and much undereducated family. He went on to study at DePauw University. He was eventually accepted at Harvard University, where he completed his graduate degree. He completed his doctorate degree in Vienna, where he started to experiment with the medical properties of soybeans. He eventually created a new drug named physostigmine, which was extremely effective at fighting the debilitating disease glaucoma, which often resulted in blindness. Thus, much of the world might be blind if not for Julian's great invention. He developed more than one hundred patents, including Aerofoam, which is used to extinguish gas and oil fires.

Julian also invented the process of synthesis. Why it that important? Synthesis was critical to the medical industry as it allowed scientists to create chemicals that were rare in nature. His work led to the birth control pill and improvements in the production of cortisone. In 2007, the PBS *Nova* series created a documentary on Julian's life called "Forgotten Genius."

Charles Richard Drew, born June 3, 1904, in Washington, DC, was the eldest of five children. He discovered that blood plasma could replace whole blood, allowing for longer storage and easier transportation. His discovery saved thousands of lives during World War II.

Otis Boykin (1920–82) invented the artificial heart pacemaker control unit. Why is that important? Although there were variations to the pacemaker before Boykin's invention, the modern-day pacemaker would not exist without his work.

James E. West (1931–present) invented the electroacoustic transducer electret microphone. Why is that important? Without James West, rappers wouldn't be able to rock the mic. West, along with Gerhard M. Sessler, helped develop the electroacoustic transducer electret microphone, for which they received a patent in 1962. Their invention was acoustically accurate, lightweight, and cost effective. Approximately 90 percent of microphones in use today—including those in telephones, tape recorders, and camcorders—are based on this original concept.

Michael Croslin, PhD, was born sometime in 1933 in the Virgin Islands. He earned many degrees, including a master's degree in electrical engineering, a doctorate in biomedical engineering, and a master's degree in business management. He fought in the army with the black Ninety-Ninth Fighter Squadron and never lost a plane. His greatest success was one of his many inventions: the computerized blood pressure device. Yes, the version that your doctor uses today is designed from his invention.

Earl D. Shaw, PhD, was born into a very poor family sometime in 1937 in Clarksdale, Mississippi, near the Hopson Plantation. His family eventually migrated to Chicago where, for the first time, he would study with whites, and he credits a white classmate for recognizing his intelligence and convincing him to go to college. He eventually earned a doctorate from the University of California—Berkeley. He became very interested in laser research and went on to coinvent "the spin-flip tunable laser," which is instrumental in the study of the chemical reactions of the body and how the body functions.

John P. Moon was born July 15, 1938, in Philadelphia. If you are working on a computer and storing information using the save command, you are probably using Moon's inventions. After working with teams of scientists at IBM, he started his own company from a garage, where he developed a magnetic substance named ferrite recording heads. His business grew rapidly, eventually becoming a multimillion-dollar business. After great success, he was contacted by Apple founders Steve Jobs and Steve Wozniak to help design and develop floppy disks and disk drives; in fact, he designed several for Apple.

George E. Carruthers, PhD, was born in a housing project on the south side of Chicago in 1939. Like Benjamin Banneker, he was very interested in space and astronomy. After college, he was hired by the Naval Research Laboratory in Washington, DC. This brought him great joy because he could now perform research in a world-class lab. He and a team of colleagues went on to invent the lunar surface ultraviolet camera/spectrograph for Apollo 16, but it was Dr. Carruthers's design, for which he received a patent. His camera made it possible to take pictures of the earth's atmosphere as well as the formation of new stars in the far distance.

Gerald A. Lawson lived from 1940 to 2011. Why is that important? Anyone who owns a PlayStation, Wii, or Xbox should know Lawson's name! He created the first home video-game system that used interchangeable cartridges, offering gamers a chance to play a variety of games and giving video-game makers a way to earn profits by selling individual games—a business model that still exists today.

Patricia Bath (1942–present) invented the cataract Laserphaco Probe. Why is that important? Her device used an innovative method of removing cataract lenses with a laser, which was more accurate than the drill-like instruments that were in common use at the time. The New York ophthalmologist's invention, patented in 1988, helped save the eyesight of millions and even restored sight to people who had been blind for more than thirty years.

Lonnie Johnson (1949–present) invented the Super Soaker. Why is that important? The Super Soaker may be a child's toy, but it is a great example of an invention with a multimillion-dollar impact. The Super Soaker generated $200 million in annual retail sales and turned the Mobile, Alabama, native into a millionaire. He's now using his fortune to develop energy technology.

George E. Alcorn (1949–present) invented the imaging X-ray spectrometer. Why is that important? The imaging X-ray spectrometer allowed scientists to examine materials that could not be broken down into smaller parts for study, revolutionizing the way NASA was able to conduct research. As a result of the significance of this work, in 1984 he was the NASA Goddard Space Flight Center Inventor of the Year. Two years later, he developed an improved method of fabrication using laser drilling.

Marc Hannah was born in 1956 in Chicago and is still alive. Why is that important? Anyone awed by the special effects in the films *Jurassic Park*, *Terminator 2*, and *The Abyss* should thank Marc Hannah. The computer scientist is one of the founders, in 1982, of the software firm Silicon Graphics (now SGI), where the special-effects genius developed 3-D graphics technology that was used in many Hollywood films.

Arthur Zang (1988–present) invented the Cardiopad. Why is that important? At the age of twenty-four, this Cameroonian engineer invented the Cardiopad, a touch-screen medical tablet that enables heart examinations, such as an electrocardiogram (ECG), to be performed at remote, rural locations while the results of the test are transferred wirelessly to specialists who can interpret them. The device spares African patients living in remote areas the trouble of having to travel to urban centers to seek medical examinations.

Ludwick Marishane (1991–present) invented DryBath. Why is that important? At age twenty-one, Ludwick Marishane developed a formula that people can use to bathe without water. DryBath is a lotion that cleanses cheaply and easily—especially important for the 2.5 billion people worldwide who lack proper access to water and sanitation. DryBath has the same effect as an antibacterial cleanser, but it's odorless and creates a biodegradable film that cleans and moisturizes the skin. Five years later, it's now available on the market. Marishane has since enrolled at the University of Cape Town in South Africa and was named the Global Student Entrepreneur of the Year in 2011.

For years, many black researchers were not able to obtain patents for their inventions because the Supreme Court had ruled that blacks did not have the right to create or invent anything because of their lack of intellect. For that reason, many important inventions became the property of their owners or other white men who could file for patents. However, some important patents and inventions by blacks did get through the US Patent office, including the trolley car, electric light, steam turbine, electric furnace, and many inventions that supported railroad concepts.

However, starting in the mid to late 1800s, there were more than five thousand meaningful patents on record as being filed by African Americans. Here are additional inventions or patents by African Americans that served to change America and the world: the skateboard, operating system fonts, propelling means for airplanes, front panel for computers, printer housing, remote control, contact lens case, fire extinguisher, folding bed, railway signal control, car brake, hydraulic jack, jack, shoe-size scanner, method and apparatus for sterilizing and storing contact lenses, process for recurving the cornea of the eye, timing device, apparatus for removing cataract lenses, combination ultrasound and laser method for removing cataract lenses, blackboard eraser, rotary engine, folding chair, furniture structure and joint, vertical-lifted portable electric furnaces and method, syringe holder with retractable needle assembly, street-sprinkler apparatus, method for selective opening of abnormal brain tissue capillaries, electronic counting apparatus, method for making flags, dental filling composition, torpedo discharge means, street sweeper, home security system, electrical switch, luggage carrier, switching device for railways, emergency landing runway, remote control vehicle system, flying machine, method for detecting and counting bacteria, trash container, medicine tray, remote-control movable fan, boat propeller, freezing temperature indicator, refrigerating method, signaling system, tonic, riding saddles, 3-D viewing glasses, oyster punching machine, player piano, child's toilet training pants, street letter box, envelope moistener, electronic ballast or lamps, pipe and cigar holder, many parts for a vehicle, mailbox, flame retardant, pliers, autopsy apparatus, compositions and method for protecting the skin from UV rays, water heater, and so much more.

Are you amazed? This list only touches on the greatness of African Americans in the shaping of American history. I encourage you to read more about our great history, because our ancestors made us proud, and they are now looking down on us asking why we are not shining like the stars that we are. It seems that our light has grown dim. Because we were educated to expect the same opportunities in life as those who enslaved us and we have found that the same opportunities do not exist for us, many of us have grown bitter and decided not to participate in our social, economic, or academic system.

It's time to realize that you were miseducated, and time that you decide to participate in our conflicted economic system. It's sad, but chances are, no matter how educated or experienced you are, you will not be embraced and accepted in the C-suite of Fortune 1000 organizations because of the color of your skin for some years to come. Get over it, and decide to create just as your forefathers did; become your own change agent. Start now and make a positive future for you, your family, and America.

You have this same genius in you as the great inventors, scientists, doctors, and educators that I wrote about. Let's commit to living and upholding the great values of our ancestors. Yes, they were awesome, and they are watching and asking why we are not upholding their legacy. Why are we slipping into entropy? It appears soon we will hit the abyss unless we turn the tide, starting today.

Lesson 9: Let Your Genius Shine

I challenge you to let your genius shine, and at the same time, I understand why it is so difficult for you to allow your star to shine. Our parents before us were forced to be what their handlers viewed as perfect, and if they were not perfect from the perspective of the handler, they were beaten, hanged, raped, or mangled until they did everything in their power to be perfect. The news gets even worse: because our parents wanted to protect us from the awful treatment they endured for years, they instilled this need for perfection in us. I can recall clearly my mother saying, "You have to work harder and be better than the white man to succeed here in America, Roy. You cannot make mistakes."

Of course, no one is perfect; even Jesus confirmed that. But because we were conditioned to believe that we had to be perfect, not just for us, but for the entire black race, we were set up for failure. This need to be perfect is a great burden that no one should have to bear. Whenever a white person fails or does some horrible deed, it is only that one person who is condemned… that one person does not represent the entire race of white Americans. Do not allow yourself to be drawn into the notion that your behavior represents the entire race of African Americans, because that is truly a weight that no one can carry.

History has proved that you are extremely intelligent, creative, and loving. Now it's time that you allow those values to control your future. There is a future coming that you must prepare your children for, so that they are ensured full participation in our great American way of life. There will be a time in the future when African Americans will have access to a power that can control the direction of America. In fact, there will come a time in the future where no one can be elected to a national office without the support of African Americans. But you must start to prepare now.

I beg those of you who are only concerned about yourselves, wealth, and other material things to wake up and get on board now. I urge those of you who are taking advantage of your brothers and sisters in any way to stop now. The gratification that you are gaining now will not help the future generation in its quest to become the most powerful people in America's national politics. Think about your children's and your family's and your friends' future… please, please stop thinking about yourselves, for you will soon be no more if you continue.

White supremacist ideology is based first and foremost on the degradation of Black bodies in order to control them. One of the best ways to instill fear in people is to terrorize them. Yet this fear is best sustained by convincing them that their bodies are ugly, their intellect is inherently underdeveloped, their culture is less civilized, and their future warrants less concern than that of other peoples.

—Cornel West

CHAPTER 10

Changing Demographic by 2050: Will You Be Ready?

My intent in this chapter is to offer you the reader and in particular black boys, and anyone else, a realistic picture of our social system—a view that most will never share with you; a view that too many of us must learn on our own, and in far too many cases, we learn it very late in life; a view that most social scientists and anthropologists are afraid to share. This is not all-inclusive, so I encourage you to continue to research and study our complicated and very complex social system.

This next-to-last chapter is an overview of our social system that is connected closely with our economic and capitalistic system, but very disconnected from our most powerful religious system; as such, the systems are in constant conflict. In fact, when individuals from other countries see us as crazy and conflicted, they might be more correct than wrong. Based on my education, life experiences, and work experiences, I will share how I view our various systems. Finally, I will discuss why 2050 will be the year of the black boys.

Let's discuss our economic and capitalistic system, but first a brief historical view.

History

African American behavior was and is systematically influenced by white America. I cannot identify the source of this statement but it explains the behavior of too many African Americans. You were "indoctrinated with the immobilizing thought of inferiority and a belief and feeling of dependence and uselessness without their guidance and confirmation of well done." Africans came to America as slaves, but they brought with them skills that had been passed down through the generations. In fact, history clearly teaches us that Ethiopia and Egypt were the leaders of civilization, and they shared their knowledge freely with Greeks, Romans, and Jews. Your ancestors came to the new land under duress, but with knowledge of designing houses and beautiful furniture and many other skills that helped to bring America to life and that ultimately made America the most modern and wealthiest nation on earth.

In fact, it is well known among the brightest scholars of anthropology and sociology that those slaves who survived the long trip across the Atlantic were exceptionally bright regarding technology. This is one reason slave owners and the government restricted education of the newly enslaved Africans, for fear that education would increase their knowledge and slaves would begin to push aggressively for their freedom and return to Africa. The plantation owners needed slave labor to support their economic machine, which was driven primarily by cotton, but peanuts and tobacco were important as well. One might say that slaves were dumbed down and then blamed for their lack of knowledge regarding reading, writing, and arithmetic in an orchestrated effort to keep them as unpaid laborers.

The saddest part of this ordeal is the fact that, over time, far too many African Americans actually bought into these lies and began to live and teach them to their offspring. However, I suppose they had little choice, because had they not succumbed to the behavior that the slave owner wanted to see, they would have been subjected to whipping, beating, raping, and the ultimate punishment of hanging. Thus, to protect their families, they behaved as demanded.

Even today, many African Americans find it difficult to believe that they are intellectually astute. As such, too many of us situate our intellect in the areas of sports, music, and acting. I applaud the genius and the creativity of our great musicians, sports players, and actors. I also celebrate the success of these very bright individuals, but we as African Americans must seek more. We must obtain seats at the financial decision-making tables. We must obtain seats in Fortune 100, 500, and 1000 C-suites. Folks, if we ever expect to achieve the equal recognition for building this country that we so dearly deserve, we desperately need math and science teachers, writing teachers, sociologists, anthropologists, lawyers, doctors, and C-suite executives. It's time to change our beliefs regarding success, and thus, change our trajectory in this great country of America. I am reminded of a statement by Marcus Aurelius in the book *Meditations* in which he writes, "Abandon all the other ambitions you cherish, or else you will never be your own master, never be independent of others or proof against passion."

Capitalism

First, consider this simple question: How is it possible that approximately 51 percent of our population is female, 18 percent Hispanic, 13 percent African American, and only about 30 percent non-Hispanic white males, and yet 97 percent of the C-suite positions in Fortune 500 companies are held by white males? The number of women in C-suite positions has improved recently to approximately 4 percent, but the number of African Americans has actually decreased in recent years to about 1 percent or less, according to a report by the *Huffington Post*.

As I stated earlier, something more troubling is occurring in the C-suites of America. One might ask the simple question: Are white males that much smarter than everyone else? Or one might ask, are white males simply better at guiding businesses to success? Simply consider the number of white males who have failed when leading Fortune 500 organizations, and again the answer is very clear. Without any research, the first question can be answered as a no, and regarding the second question, there is a growing amount of research that clearly documents the fact that organizations are more profitable when they have women and minorities in C-suite positions and on their boards. So again I ask the simple question, how is it possible that in 2016, the C-suites of Fortune 500 companies can remain almost completely void of women and minorities?

Understanding the distribution of power and wealth was a burning question for me even early in life, but I did not know how to articulate the question in the early years. Allow me to tell you about three true stories that I actually lived—stories that started me questioning our social system and its unfairness to people of color.

I wrote about this earlier, but it is important enough to review. When I was in the air force, I worked for an African American colonel who reported to a major in the dental services. As we all know, a colonel outranks a major, but in this case, he was second-in-command. I often wondered, how is that possible? Eventually I asked Dr. English why he reported to a major. He preferred not to discuss it in much detail, but simply stated, "You will learn, Roy." He became one of my mentors in the air force, and we shared time together with our families. He was instrumental in teaching me and my family some points of social etiquette that we were not fortunate enough to learn in our environment while growing up in Memphis. He taught us simple etiquette, such as how to set a table properly and how to eat properly. He also taught me about dress and communication. Because of him, I went on to become the noncommissioned officer in charge of the base dental services.

The second story is about after I left Target stores and the board determined to promote the executive senior vice president of marketing and merchandising to the chief executive officer's position versus some other much more qualified internal executive candidates. In my opinion, this guy was not a very bright individual, and he demonstrated signs of being insensitive to minorities, particularly African Americans. He would go on to virtually destroy an organization that was on the cutting edge of retail, technology, and growth. I ask the question: How is it possible that some white men can consistently demonstrate incompetent performance and still be promoted to top-level executive positions? This scenario is repeated again and again in many Fortune 500 organizations.

Finally, when I joined Jewel-Osco, it was with the promise that I would be promoted to vice president in a short while, and the commitment was realized. In one short year, my performance and results proved to be exceptional, and because of my results I was promised a senior vice president position as soon as one opened. However, after I was in the position as a vice president for a short while, the organization changed hands, some leadership changes were made, and the senior vice president of operations was promoted to president.

On his very first full day in the position, he called me into his office and told me that the company was going in a different direction and that I would not be promoted to senior vice president. He went on to add, "You will be moving from the north area to lead the South Side of Chicago." This was an area that his best friend had screwed up for years. Though I liked this individual as a person, it was clear that, intellectually, he did not have the capacity to lead a $6 billion organization in Chicago. In fact, many of his close friends echoed the same concern in private.

Shortly after his promotion, he made a decision that baffled almost everyone in the organization. He decided to throw Starbucks out of the Jewel-Osco stores. The executive staff was in shock. How does one throw Starbucks out of their stores? Because he wanted control of the Starbucks shops that were in his stores and Starbucks said hell no, he told them to leave. It was funny that after the very day he demanded that Starbucks leave, they removed all of their equipment from the stores before daylight the next day. That was the day that I decided to plan my exit strategy to leave Jewel-Osco, and about one year after that, I did leave. Just two short years after I left, he had virtually destroyed a one-hundred-year Chicago success story single-handedly.

Again I ask myself, how is it possible that these three men from three different times in my life and three different parts of America could be anointed to lead organizations when they were much less qualified than many others in the organization, and two of the three destroyed organizations that were previously very successful?

I offer this theory, with some supporting documentation. It is my opinion that the only way this is possible is that many Fortune 500 companies are controlled from the C-suite and the board willfully by either white supremacists or implicitly by others using and accessing misleading heuristics. One does not need months and years of research or education to grasp my premise regarding the makeup of the C-suite. In fact, I believe my assertion is easily supported by the demographic data I reviewed earlier and the fact that research has proven that organizations with diverse senior executive leadership are more profitable. Tell me, how else can anyone explain the phenomenon that 97 percent of all C-suite executives are white men? Personally, I think that women make better leaders than men at every executive level for many reasons, but this book does not allow the space for that argument.

Now, it should be clear that our economic system is driven by the 97 percent who control the leadership positions in corporate America. Knowing that fact should cause the vast majority of Americans to stop blaming anyone but these guys for jobs leaving America and low wages. Stop blaming Latinos and other minorities for taking jobs. Folks, jobs in America are controlled by the 97 percent in the C-suites, and they are not minorities. The demographics in Fortune 500 companies offer us the perfect picture of our capitalistic system. The primary focus of capitalism is to create and control wealth, and based on the makeup of the individuals leading Fortune 500 companies, there are at least three beliefs that these Fortune 500 leaders hold:

1. There is an implicit or explicit belief that white men should control the vast majority of America's capital.
2. There is an implicit or explicit belief that white men are the only ones with the intellect to manage and lead Fortune 500 companies because of the amount of wealth involved.
3. There is an implicit belief that white men deserve wealth no matter their abilities.

Thus, to my mind, the word "capitalism," to some degree, means that the majority of the capital available is controlled by the 97 percent of white male executives in Fortune 500 companies, and all others, including the proletariats of our society, are the means by which they drive their wealth.

I am reminded of the time recently that I had lunch with a city councilman from a major city. He started a conversation about those who are on welfare, stating, "We have to get those people off welfare and get them to work. They are a drain on the city and our budgets." During that same conversation he said, and I quote, "I have the best job in the world. I have a nice office, a great assistant, I make good money, and I don't have to do anything but a few meetings a year. What a great country." Now this guy had just finished saying that people on welfare were bad people, and in the same conversation he said that it was OK for him to take welfare from the city. He is so privileged that he does not recognize that he is taking advantage of our social system in a much worse way than many of those hungry individuals who are on welfare.

Religious System

One cannot understand our social system without having some knowledge about our religious system. In previous years, from the time we entered grade school, our religious conditioning began with reciting the Pledge of Allegiance. We can all recall learning and reciting every word, every day of school. Many of us went to church, and we were further indoctrinated with deep beliefs regarding the Bible. In fact, I hold many religious views even today.

However, our capitalistic system is in major conflict with much of the teachings of the books in the Bible. For example, our capitalistic system is all about creating wealth for very few; and much of the Bible, particularly the New Testament, teaches us that we are our brother's keeper, and while the poor will be with us always, we should offer helping hands. Our capitalistic system teaches just the opposite. It teaches us that those who have not achieved wealth, or at least a degree of independence that some wealth brings, have not worked hard enough or are lazy and so on, when, in fact, many of the executives that I have engaged who occupy the C-suites are no worthier of holding a position in a C-suite than many of the bright homeless people I have met on the streets of Chicago, Houston, LA, and San Francisco. In fact, many of those homeless people would do a much better job than some of the dummies I have met who lead Fortune 500 organizations. Thus, you find many of these Fortune 500 leaders praying to their God on Sunday and praying to their capital on Monday. Given this situation, we as Americans are constantly torn between church, state, and capital.

Preparing for 2050

By the year 2050, our population will approach 400 million; the white male population minus the Hispanics who claim to be white in the US Census will be approximately 23 percent of the population versus today's 30 percent. In fact, some demographic studies have the white male population as low as 18 percent in 2050, and about 77 percent, or 71 million, will be of voting age. White men are also the older population. The Hispanic population will grow from almost 18 percent in 2015 to 27 percent or more in 2050. Currently, 44 percent of the Hispanic population are 18 or older, and that number is small when compared to white Americans and African Americans. However, they are the youngest, with a median age of 27.6, and they have 26 percent of all babies younger than the age of 1. Accordingly, their voting-age population will grow at a faster rate than all others by the year 2050. However, for this analysis, I will hold the voting-age population to 73 percent: the same as African Americans, or approximately 77 million voters. Based on current voting trends, white men will continue to lean right, and Hispanics will lean left; because of that divided trajectory, African Americans and white women will have the opportunity to decide all general elections starting in 2050 or earlier.

The African American population is currently about 13 percent of the total population, but it is estimated that because of interracial marriage, African Americans will comprise 16 percent or more of the population by 2050. Two-thirds or 73 percent of the African American population is aged eighteen or older, and that number will remain fairly consistent; therefore, about 41 million will be eligible to vote in 2050, and since about 40 percent of the eligible voters actually vote, that is about 17 million votes. White females will make up approximately 24 percent of the population in 2050. Currently, roughly 79 percent are of voting age. Should that number hold true for the year 2050, about 75 million will be eighteen or older, and they vote at a rate of 46 percent. However, their population is expected to decline because of the lower birthrate. The good news is that white women continue to find their voice, a voice that champions fairness for their kids and yours. As such, one can expect that the majority will vote for what is right for all American people, and that will serve you, African Americans, well, too, but you must vote.

The bottom line is that African Americans will have a much stronger voice in helping to decide the outcome of national elections. However, the voting age population is the key to America's democracy. Consider this analysis, which predicts the voting age population for the year 2050. Historically, 45 percent of white men who are eligible to vote actually vote, and if that number holds true, they would have about 32 million votes to cast. Let's give them 90 percent of that vote or 29 million votes. Recall that white women will have about 75 million eligible voters, and 46 percent will vote. Thus, they will have 36 million votes to cast. Let's split their vote evenly at 50 percent. That would give Democrats and Republicans 18 million votes each. For argument sake, let's give one percent of the African-American vote to the conservative party. Let's assume that Hispanics continue their support of liberal views, and if so, because of the number of births, they will have about 68 million eligible voters, but historically, they have a very low turnout rate of 27 percent; if that rate should continue, about 18 million will vote in 2050. Let's give the Republican party 15% of the Hispanic votes in 2050 or approximately 3 million votes. Asians will have about 24 million votes. However, only 27% of eligible Asian voters cast votes, so the total is about 6.5 million, split equally between Republicans and Democrats. That would give the Republicans approximately 53 million, or 28 percent, of the votes, and that assumes that they would take 90 percent of white men's votes, which is improbable. For example, the Republicans received 26.3 percent of the eligible vote in 2016, and Democrats received 26.5 percent. Let's consider that there will be approximately 290,000,000 eligible voters but only about 65%, or 188 million, will register and, traditionally, fewer of the total number vote. For argument's sake, let's give the Democrats 28 percent, or the same 53 million votes, and assume that about 83 million eligible voters will be unaccounted for.

With the remaining 83 million potential voters, the Democrats or Republicans could easily carry every national election with the support of the African American vote. However, two major problems must be addressed. First, we will have about ten to fifteen million African American citizens who are eligible to vote, but they will not even register to vote. Another two million or more will be in prison unless we turn that around now. Should 90% of the eligible African American voters determine to exercise their power of the vote, they will be incredibly powerful. In 2050, the Democratic Party or the Republican Party will win virtually every national election if they can swing the vast majority of the African American vote. I would argue that, because of the Hispanic growth in America, the Republicans will need the African American vote more than the Democrats so as to win any national election. So, African Americans must be open to the party that demonstrates their commitments to helping improve the lives of all African Americans. So too, we must find ways and methods to keep our brothers out of prison so they can cast their votes for our American Democracy.

Please, I beg of you to share this information with all people. You will probably never hear this from anyone else before the year 2050. Black boys, this is an awesome power to hold. Just think: you will have the power to swing elections your way. Now that's real power, but are you ready?

Based on the current state of too many African Americans, I would argue that you need to prepare for the power you will hold in 2050 by focusing on the following areas: education, mentoring, and business.

Education is, of course, the big equalizer and must be our number-one priority. So, too, we need to become experts in understanding how our economic system works. Please add the study of economics to your kids' education agenda. Here you will learn how to grow in a system that is very complicated and has basically been reserved for the affluent. Second, study history—African American history, American history, and the history of Africa. It's a shame to say, but because our educational system has chosen not to teach the true history of African Americans, you must, of necessity, teach yourself, your kids, and your entire family. Your history is a rich history, filled with inventors, strategists, mathematicians, doctors, lawyers, politicians, and many scientists. As I stated earlier, there could be no civilized America without African American inventors, scientists, doctors, and laborers. Teach your kids our great history and make them proud.

Let's all become mentors. I am so enamored with the Latinos and Asian population because of their great sense of support for one another. Their goal is to lift one another up no matter where they are in life. Their goal is to mentor and give one another jobs and to share success together. I am oftentimes saddened because of the way we treat one another—yes, I can be found occasionally shedding tears of sadness. When we should be mentoring and supporting one another, too many of us join the majority and the media and behave just as we have been trained since slavery; we start pointing fingers and saying, "I told you so."

It is very heartbreaking to see how our so-called black leaders such as Jesse Jackson and others have simply used African Americans to fill their own pockets with great wealth. Just look at Jackson's hometown of Chicago. While he has become a very wealthy man, the kids on the South Side of Chicago are killing one another.

I also call on our churches to step up and become mentors and better supporters of our lost kids. Folks, I am all for praying, but let's spend more time *doing* something in the communities. Teach the kids about their greatness; help them to get a good education and start small businesses.

Finally, brothers, just as the Latinos and Asians have done so well, let's start our own businesses and share but not yield our storefronts to newcomers. Far too often Asians, Middle Easterners, and others open businesses in our neighborhood when we have the same knowledge and capacity to do so. Again, let's share and embrace our brothers from other lands, but start helping one another as well. Your ancestors were leaders in small businesses, and they were not afraid of personal success. In other words, they were OK if Fortune 500 companies left them out because they had their own successful businesses and they cherished their independence. There are business mentors out there, but you must seek them out. Just as the Bible says in Luke 11:9, "So I say to you, ask, and it will be given to you; seek, and you will find; knock, and it will be opened to you."

Whatever you do, if you are one of my brothers who is poisoning our young people, please stop today, because 2050 will be here before we know it, and you must be prepared for a power that you have not had previously.

If you are one of my brothers who is killing and fighting because you believe that life has nothing else to offer, please know that you are wrong. Life is waiting for you to give it the space to reveal your true purpose. Brothers, if you do not stop and listen to the universe, you will never realize your real life purpose, and believe me, your life purpose is about joy, happiness, and great wealth, if that is what your heart desires. Yes, you can have great wealth, joy, and happiness without hurting and destroying the lives and futures of your brothers and sisters.

Those are the three keys…education, mentoring, and becoming business savvy. With those three you can prepare for your greatness in 2050.

Lesson 10: You Can Be a Hero, Too

Now listen to this carefully. You were made wonderfully in the very image of our almighty God, and it is time that all of us start to live up to God's expectations of us and our abilities. Start with honoring all women, particularly women of color. Just as white men have placed white women on the highest pedestal of all, particularly those with blond hair and blue eyes, you must place women of color on a higher pedestal.

By the way, let's all agree to stop using these ugly, socially constructed terms such as black people, white people, and so on. We are one human race; we just happen to be different beautiful shades of color, just as the leaves of the trees. But we didn't name the various trees by the color of their leaves. We named them by their precious fruit, or strength, as in the oak tree. This whole notion of race and color is in place to support social separation for power and capital, so let's agree to begin to move away from the bondage of those ugly, separating terms.

Understand that much of the news cycle is dependent on the small amount of demeaning news the media find in our neighborhoods and the destructive behavior that some brothers perpetrate on others for their viewers and their capital. The sad thing is that the news cycles are for those who have the financial ability to support the media by buying the products advertisers display on the news and on most commercial programs; by and large, those are white females.

Brothers, let's commit today to stop allowing the media to sell billions of dollars of products because of the poor behavior of some people of color. Let's commit today: we are not going to allow the wealthy the opportunity to make billions on our backs. Brothers, you are still being treated as slaves when you represent the behavior that allows the media to sell products and demean an entire people in the process. Just as the wealthy made millions by working our ancestors from sunup to sundown picking cotton and tobacco, they are now making billions by portraying you as the bad guy, and thereby convincing Fortune 1000 organizations and small business owners that you are not worthy of professional jobs—even though only a small minority of our brothers behave in ways that are hurtful to others.

One might say that based on the makeup of the executive suites in America, African Americans have been virtually excluded from meaningful jobs. However, I would argue that the media have helped to create an ugly image of black males, and far too many of the majority, and some people of color, are buying into a corrupt media led by, you guessed it, billionaires. Let's not give them one more single ugly piece of news to advertise that is representative of people of color.

Let's commit to forcing the media to find other ways to scare the general public into spending billions on advertised products. Let's make it known that no longer will they be able to make billions at the expense of African Americans. Let's seek out ways to get women and others to help us fight the news and media that consistently run demeaning broadcasts focused on African Americans. They air the news as representative of an entire people, when in fact, vast numbers of serious crimes are committed by the majority here in America.

Let's commit to forcing the media to change their advertising ways, and let's work hard to get good, fair-minded Americans to join our fight against the media. Let's commit to highlighting those companies and manufacturers that support such poor taste in advertising, just for profit, on the backs of people of color. Let's commit to damaging their profits, just as they have committed to damaging the character of generations of people of color by highlighting a few destructive acts as representative of all people of color.

It's ironic that when one or a group from the majority commits hideous acts of violence, it's never representative of an entire people. It is only that crazy individual. We can change the way the media and some others from the majority have colored the minds of the world about people of color. If we do nothing else, let's not offer them any way to make a single dime by exploiting our communities in a bad way. Stop it now; stop today.

Your friends shape your world, so choose wisely. You will become a product of your environment unless you resist the many unfavorable temptations around you. Too many of you are in an environment that is not positive, but you can become passionate about reading, researching, and volunteering. Give of yourself.

Do not allow yourself to become a product of your environment. Seek out ways to visit parks, museums, and different churches. I enjoy church, because that's where I find a few hours of total peace. That's where I generate new ideas and start the week with a healthy attitude. Even if you are in a negative environment, there is always someone around who just seems to transcend the negative and walk away with a successful and healthy life. Find that person, and speak with him or her often. Mirror what he or she is doing, and you can begin to grow from there.

> My aim is not to provide excuses for Black behavior or to absolve Blacks of personal responsibility. But when the new Black conservatives accent Black behavior and responsibility in such a way that the cultural realities of Black people are ignored, they are playing a deceptive and dangerous intellectual game with the lives and fortunes of disadvantaged people. We indeed must criticize and condemn immoral acts of Black people, but we must do so cognizant of the circumstances into which people are born and under which they live. By overlooking these circumstances, the new Black conservatives fall into the trap of blaming Black poor people for their predicament. It is imperative to steer a course between the Scylla of environmental determinism and the Charybdis of a blaming-the-victim's perspective.
>
> —CORNEL WEST, *RACE MATTERS*

CHAPTER 11

Reflections

I DECIDED TO END MY book with reflections from Africa because I wanted to share my life-changing event with you as a last experience in reading my book. It is one that all Americans should experience, particularly African Americans. Once you have visited the homeland, you will be a changed person for life, changed in very positive ways. You will come to understand what real love is for all people no matter their race, gender, sexual preference, background, or history.

GHANA

To better understand our conflicted social system, one must experience the culture of another country on a different continent, and for black boys, I suggest the continent of Africa. I had on my wish list the dream to visit Africa, and in 2009 that dream was realized. This trip to the country of Ghana, and the city of Accra, was the most mentally refreshing experience I ever had in my life. I discovered that the pictures of African life that we had been shown and the ugly history of much of Africa were simply not true. I learned many facts about America and our socialization process. I learned that much of the history that we were taught in school about Africa was simply fabricated to support the privileged beliefs about those who had been enslaved—our ancestors, Africans.

Although I would like to debate the African American socialization process into the American slavery culture, this book is not the place for that debate. However, it should be made clear to you that much of the text in the K–12 schoolbooks regarding the African slave trade or the socialization process of Africans is either totally fabricated or simply omits the truth. I suppose telling the truth about the treatment of Africans is too painful for those whose ancestors either committed the acts, supported the acts, or were told about the awful treatment of Africans…brutal treatment in the name of capital, power, and control. If you desire to disconnect from the powerful American socialization process, you must experience your native land.

While working on my undergraduate degree, I took a class titled Modern African History, and my team selected Ghana as the country we wanted to explore. We studied their culture, their food, their education, their beliefs, and more. I was so taken by this experience that I made it an absolute personal requirement to visit Ghana, Africa. In early 2009, I began to speak to my family about traveling to Ghana, and they all refused to join me. And so I began to plan my trip alone. I selected my hotel, planned my tours, and began to share my upcoming trip plans with my family.

After seeing the hotel, my youngest daughter and my wife both said, "You did not tell us that you were staying in a five-star hotel!" They had visions in their minds that our African brothers and sisters were animals and very dangerous—visions that our social system had driven so deep into their psyches that they could not and would not believe or even imagine that Ghana was a safe place.

To prove that Accra was safe, I placed a call to our US embassy in Ghana, and I spoke with the captain in charge. I asked him to tell me about the potential dangers in Accra. These are his words exactly: "Where do you live in America?" I stated, "We live in the Chicago area." He then stated, "Well, the south side of Chicago is much more dangerous than Accra." He further stated, "You are safe here, and the only danger is that if you lay your wallet down, someone might take it." He continued, "We have no murders, no robberies, and no gang fights. You will be safe."

I think it's time that you experience Ghana through my eyes. Here, then, is my day-by-day account of my visit to Ghana—a visit that changed me forever by bringing an unconditional love into my heart for all people and helped to put my socialization process here in America into a global perspective, not just an American perspective.

The Beginning!

This is the beginning of a lifelong dream…our trip to Ghana, Africa! This memoir represents years of dreams and months of planning to visit the homeland.

This visit to Africa exceeded all my expectations, and to date, is one of the most wondrous events of my life. I wish that you find the following pages both educational and inspiring. Enjoy Accra, Ghana, located on the continent of Africa!

> May peace and love bring the world together as one,
> so that we humans never again allow any living being
> to suffer such pain as slavery and the slave trade.
>
> —Roy Whitmore

Day 1

October 15, 2009

As I reflect on this exciting journey back to the homeland, I find myself somewhat emotional, and in a sense, a bit fearful of what I might see or encounter in terms of this new experience as compared to my American life. I cannot believe that I am going back to where it all began.

My daughter asks, why not Ethiopia? Because, based on her research, my ancestors most likely began their trip to the West from there.

The answer is simple. I studied the great historical nation of Ghana in undergrad school. What an experience! After the many weeks of research of Ghana's history, including their politics, culture, food, religion, and more, I was in love with the country. As such, I am now fulfilling a longtime dream.

It is a bit strange to me that, as I write this, I have no complete vision or expectations of what I might experience in Ghana. Maybe I feel that I will be accepted just for me…I will not be judged because of my skin, and I will finally be home. We are in O'Hare awaiting our flight to New York City.

October 16, 2009

We are on the flight to Ghana, and I note that it is 1:00 a.m. central time in Chicago and 6:00 a.m. central time in Accra. It is early morning on the Delta flight, and I suppose I have just awakened to daylight. I am amazed at my comfort among the many people on this flight. It is a very large plane—I suppose a jumbo jet. As I look across the plane, I note that 99 percent of the people look like me. They are the same shade. They are all so friendly and respectful of one another. Momentarily my mind drifts, and I wonder how so many African Americans became so disrespectful. I wonder what sociological theory might apply. I relax again and realize that we are now over the continent of Africa. I imagine that we are crossing the northwestern part of Africa, now flying over Morocco or the Western Sahara.

I overhear someone speak fondly about President Obama, and I smile. I relax and await our arrival with a deep feeling of anticipation. I am not sure what I will encounter, but for some reason I have yet to construct in my mind a visual of what I expect or wish to see.

We arrive at our beautiful hotel!

Day 2
October 17, 2009

I am amazed at how the long flight has affected me. I suppose I expected that I would just naturally adjust. I did not sleep very much on the plane, and I feel tired with the need for rest; however, my excitement easily overcomes any fatigue.

Although the lobby is beautiful and could be rated a five-star, the room is a three-star at best. However, it is very clean, and the service is five-star.

I am relaxing now, and reflecting back to yesterday and the drive from the airport. I became a bit uncomfortable because there were so many people attempting to sell us their products. I recall that Ghana is an open market, and this is their mode of entrepreneurship. I made a special mental note…I did not feel threatened in this situation as I might have in some communities back in America. In fact, I wanted to buy something from each of them. My wife and daughter saved me from purchasing things that we did not need.

As the day progresses, I begin to notice that everyone we encounter or notice from a distance appears to be very happy. But how could they be happy when they have so little?

This would become my thesis.

I also noted that everyone had a very soft handshake. I wondered if I should be reaching out to shake hands, and I pondered whether the people had become subservient because of the many years of occupation by several nations. After all, they only obtained their freedom from Britain fifty-two years ago.

It has been a long day, and we have just completed a very good dinner. Each of us noted that the food was void of the salt and sugar we have come to expect in America. After dinner, I determine to relax and reflect as I do back home, all alone. However, I realize that one reason I am here is to learn about the structure of the organizations here in Ghana. I begin to introduce myself to the managers and leaders of the Hotel Labadi. This hotel reminds me so much of the hotel highlighted in the movie *Hotel Rwanda*. An uncomfortable feeling touches me for just an instant.

I meet Dominic, one of the managers of the hotel, and I engage him in a deep conversation about the structure of the hotel. I learn that the organizational structure of the hotel is not that different from American organizations, but there is one major difference: their hotel is owned by the government.

Day 3
October 18, 2009

This is an eye-opener of a day. Today is the first day of our tours. We meet our tour guide, Eric. He is quiet at first, but warms up to us quickly.

We visit the International Conference Center. The center is home to the Non-Aligned Movement. This is an association of developing countries that have decided not to align themselves with one particular country.

Next we visit Accra's oldest neighborhood, James Town, which continues to be a fishing harbor even today. The people seem very happy. My mind drifts, and I ask, how could this be under these harsh circumstances? I am now thinking—James Town was bustling with energy. Although the homes are but shacks, I found the town to be very clean, as were the people. In fact, the people were generally well dressed and happy.

The fishing quarters could be considered an old shacktown, but again, the people did not appear to be angry. Now my concern shifts to their social development. The highlight of the day was the visit to the Dr. W. E. B. DuBois Memorial Centre. I found myself standing in the center of his library, family room, bedroom, and kitchen. I am amazed!

I seemed to feel the pain of Dr. DuBois's many years of struggle for equal rights for African Americans. There were books in his library with small white page identifiers still in place.

His house in Accra, which was given to him by the government of Accra, contains many of his books and other artifacts. I wish all African Americans could experience this for their personal growth. I did indeed feel his presence.

We toured much of the remainder of the city and found, as would be expected, that the American and the British embassies were the largest and most modern of all.

Another famous sight for today was Kwame Nkrumah Memorial Park (KNMP). I was lost in the world of this great African leader. He was Ghana's first president, elected in 1960, and he is responsible for their relatively advanced state of democracy today. There were teachers with young elementary-age students teaching them their African history. It was such a joy for me to watch them learn about their great nation as they laughed, played, and shared.

We visited many other sites, including a grocery store, which was not unlike what is just down the street back home.

Day 4
October 19, 2009

I think we are starting to adjust to the time change, although we are finding it difficult to sleep at night. However, we are so excited that sleep really does not matter now.

Today we are scheduled for a boat cruise on the Volta River. This is the largest manmade lake in the world. Not sure why they call it a riverboat cruise when it is on a lake.

The cruise was wonderful, and the lake is beautiful, with a nice breeze until late afternoon, when the heat became almost unbearable. The cruise hosted a very diverse group of people, most from other parts of the world.

I did note one important difference in behavior on the boat. The German, Indian, Japanese, and other visitors were very respectful. However, the white Americans offered very little respect, as they were running through the boat, jumping the dinner line, and generally being very loud. I wondered about the assertive behavior of the Americans as opposed to that of others on the boat, particularly the Africans.

The tour was too long in light of the extreme heat toward the end of the day, although as we docked, we encountered some kids welcoming us back with fun chatter. It was another educational day!

Day 5
October 20, 2009
A rest day!

Day 6

October 21, 2009

Today is a most exciting day. We are off to a Torgorme naming ceremony. We will meet the paramount chief and elders, and also participate in a naming ceremony, where we will be given our traditional African names.

All I can say is, "Wow!" This is absolutely unbelievable. We are greeted as if we are long-lost family, and I suppose that truly is the case.

We were made to feel most comfortable. The kids wanted to hug and be hugged…I was in heaven.

The names given to us are as follows: My first name is Kawame, "born on Saturday," and my surname is Dzidefo, a local surname meaning courage. Dot's first name is Awysi, "born on Sunday," and her surname is Kokoe, meaning holy. Quendrida's first name is Adza, "born on Monday," and her surname is Sika, meaning gold.

We were all given bracelets and a cup as a gift. I had to give an acceptance speech, and I promised to send them a computer. (I later sent them two.) We all danced and enjoyed the day. I recall having a stomach problem as we arrived, but once we were greeted with all the joy, it disappeared.

Only pictures and video can express our joy better. How could they be so happy?

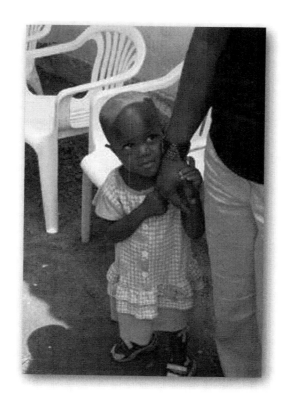

Day 7
October 22, 2009

It is early, and I am reflecting on what might happen today as we prepare to visit the Cape Coast and Elmina Castles. Although there were slaveholding stations up and down the Gold Coast, the most prolific sites were these two. We are very quiet as we take the two-hour drive north up the coast toward the Cape Coast.

We visited Elmina Castle first. This is the largest of the castles, built in 1482 by the Portuguese. It is also known as Saint George Castle. This was the first of the castles to be built in sub-Saharan Africa. It is said that as many as twelve million slaves passed through this castle. Half of them died on location, and more died on the seas. However, I believe that that number is far below the actual number that passed through here and died here and en route to the

New World. It seems that I can still smell death four hundred years later. I am humbled as I enter the compound, almost not noticing the bright young kids asking our names—and not realizing that these young kids would have a pleasant surprise in store for us when we exited the compound. They offered each of us a seashell with our names, their names, and an e-mail address.

Originally established as a trading post for liquor, guns, and other items, the castles became slaveholding compounds because the West and European countries were becoming more industrialized and needed cheap labor. In fact, the Portuguese found that slave trading was more lucrative than trading gold.

We learned that Africans were selected for different reasons than we had been led to believe back in America. They were selected because they were skilled farmers, used advanced farming tools, were very healthy with no visible illnesses, and were generally bigger and stronger than their European counterparts.

Facts: The Portuguese held slaves on the Gold Coast for 155 years, the Dutch for 235 years, and the British for eighty-five years. Ghana has been free for only fifty-two years. Now, as one of the most advanced countries in Africa, it embraces democracy as a way of life.

The Africans were subjected to all types of indignities and tortures. As many as nine hundred men would be held in one small room for months (see below) with little food and no facilities.

I am sickened by much of what the tour guide is telling us. In fact, Dot is ill and cannot continue at the Cape Coast Castle tour. She tells us that she is too hot, but I sense that it is the smell of death and the sound of torture in this sacred place, for after all, she is the holy one. It seems that you can actually feel the pain and see the destruction in real time.

Misled

The women were routinely raped; should they refuse, they were tortured. Cannonballs were chained to their ankles, and they were left in the sun for hours until they submitted or passed out. Should they continue to refuse, they were locked in a separate small room (see below) until they died.

Men who refused to obey orders were locked in dungeons with no food or water until they died, and then they were tossed into the ocean.

I am asking myself, how could people be so barbaric? I am now beginning to understand how white America could treat African Americans so inhumanely because they were taught well by history. I am beginning to wonder why the African people are not upset with the British, Dutch, Portuguese, and others that imprisoned them and literally looted much of their wealth in terms of gold, diamonds, and the most valuable of all, their human capital.

I now understand why we (African Americans) are greeted with open arms here. It is because they want their most valuable treasure back home… they want us back. The door below is the Door of No Return, and once you entered, you either died or went West or to a European country.

Misled

It was hurtful to learn that half of the Africans who were held in these castles died there, and half of those who survived that imprisonment died en route to their final destination. It should be noted that those who survived this awful experience were indeed mentally and physically strong.

What was most sick about these horrific events is that, while men and women oftentimes lay dying below, those who perpetrated these acts engaged themselves in parties above.

Same-Day Reflections

As I reflect and think this through, it appears to me that the African people are subservient in a way that today is an implicit cognitive development. After only fifty-two years of freedom, what would one expect? How many years will it take for the African people to realize their true worth, just like the newly awakening Chinese?

After 475 years of occupation, my African brothers and sisters have been conditioned to display a subservient and most respectful behavior, lest they suffer the awful consequences of their human behavior, desires, and needs. Again, what sociological theory can explain their behavior, their human development over the years?

I feel the need to help through education or funding. I now feel a connection to my homeland that I could not have felt before this remarkable trip. This has indeed been my greatest learning experience, and I know that my personal transformation has just begun as a result of this historic trip. Finally, I am thankful and so very happy that Dot and Quendrida joined me. I wish that La Juana and RJ had come. Wow!

FINAL REFLECTIONS

I AM HOME NOW, AND I continue to be in awe of our magnificent trip to Africa. I have many stories to tell, including meeting the general who led the overthrow of Idi Amin, the onetime Ugandan dictator and leader. They asked me to come home to Uganda and teach leadership in one of the universities, and I think that would be a privilege.

My most fun memory was visiting the Torgorme naming ceremony. What wonderful, bright people, and the kids are all love. I am now disturbed at myself because I had such low expectations of my African family. They are very intelligent people, and their friendly behavior is most captivating. It is so natural. They are indeed the enlightened ones.

Though one of the original purposes of the trip was to study organizational structures, after just a few days, I quickly found myself most concerned with their social structure, their human development, and their engaging, loving behavior.

How could a people who were held in captivity for over four hundred years be so kind and embracing of those who committed inhuman acts of slavery against them? I will return.

Certainly visiting your homeland will shed some light on the American socialization process of black boys. As such, I encourage you to visit Africa right away. In Ghana, you will not see the violence that you see on our television networks and in the news constantly. You will not see one race of people compared against another in an effort to demean one while building up another. You will not see advertisers spending billions of dollars on negative, degrading news to capture the attention of those who have the most spending power.

In schools, you will find that African history is taught realistically, but in a context that does not call for violence against anyone. In fact, I asked dozens of Ghanaians to explain how they could embrace a people such as the British, French, and Spaniards—people who raped their women and robbed them blind of their wealth. In each response, I heard no bitterness. Each one simply stated, "That was then, and this is now. We welcome all people as equals to our land." Even as I write this, I am amazed at such a positive attitude. I am moved by such caring for all people, even by a people who were enslaved for hundreds of years.

THE END: QUOTES

I WISH TO END MY book with some of my favorite quotes and a couple poems that I wrote.

> Where justice is denied, where poverty is enforced, where ignorance prevails, and where any one class is made to feel that society is in an organized conspiracy to oppress, rob, and degrade them, neither persons nor property will be safe.
>
> —FREDERICK DOUGLASS, SPEECH ON THE TWENTY-FOURTH ANNIVERSARY OF EMANCIPATION IN WASHINGTON, DC

> I am an invisible man…I am a man of substance, of flesh and bone, fiber and liquids—and I might even be said to possess a mind. I am invisible, understand, simply because people refuse to see me.
>
> —RALPH ELLISON, *INVISIBLE MAN*

> Herein lies the tragedy of the age: not that men are poor—all men know something of poverty; not that men are wicked—who is good? Not that men are ignorant—what is truth? Nay, but that men know so little of men.
>
> —W. E. B. DuBois, *THE SOULS OF BLACK FOLK*

> We are not fighting for integration, nor are we fighting for separation. We are fighting for recognition as human beings…In fact, we are actually fighting for rights that are even greater than civil rights and that is human rights.
>
> —Malcolm X, "Black Revolution" speech

I wrote the following poem in 1972 while in the US Air Force leading the diversity committee.

> Life is a struggle for people like me, for people with black skin just like me. We were murdered, raped, and stripped of our rights. Those people who did this, you know, are white. The black has pulled through slavery and oppression but still must fight for any satisfaction. They say we are free and have all rights. If this is true, then why must we fight? Some white men behave like nothing but boys and have treated the black man as automatic toys.
>
> But the Black is advancing very fast, and the white man is afraid that he will soon live the past.
>
> —Roy Whitmore

Life is a gift not to be held, but to be shared without strings and things. No, life is glory, or is it a story to be told to all without any motive? No, maybe life is the past, no, could it be the future, but without the present what good can it do you? Yes, life is a gift for all to share, not on your terms, sir, or have you not learned? Yes, life is a gift and not one for us to keep; it's meant to be shared before our deep sleep.

—Roy Whitmore

REFERENCES

Adams, B. D., L. Rehak, A. A. Brown, and C. T. Hall. *Human Decision-Making Biases*. Report produced for Defense Research and Development Canada. Guelph, Ontario: HumanSystems, 2009.

Beckner, Chrisanne. *100 African-Americans Who Shaped American History*. San Mateo, CA: Bluewood Books, 1995.

DuBois, W. E. B. *The Souls of Black Folk*. New York: Barnes & Noble, 1903.

Embrick, D. G. "The Diversity Ideology in the Business World: A New Oppression for a New Age." *Critical Sociology, 37*(5) (2011): 541–56.

History.com. "Slavery in America." A+E Networks. 2009. http://www.history.com/topics/Black-history/slavery.

The History Guy. Roger Lee. 2016. http://www.historyguy.com.

Hudson, Wade. *Book of Black Heroes: Scientists, Healers, and Inventors (Volume 3)*. East Orange, NJ: Just Us Books, 1897.

Pew Research Center. "African Immigrant Population in U.S. Steadily Climbs." Monica Anderson. February 14, 2017. http://www.pewresearch.org/fact-tank/2017/02/14/african-immigrant-population-in-u-s-steadily-climbs/.

The Root. "How Many Slaves Landed in the US?" Henry Lewis Gates Jr. January 6, 2014. http://www.theroot.com/articles/history/2014/01/how_many_slaves_came_to_america_fact_vs_fiction/.

Sluby, Patricia Carter. *The Inventive Spirit of African Americans: Patented Ingenuity.* Westport, CT: Praeger Publishing, 2008.

Sluby, Patricia Carter. *The Entrepreneurial Spirit of African American Inventors.* Santa Barbara, CA: Praeger Publishing, 2011.

Smith, Jessie Carney. *Black Firsts: 4,000 Ground-Breaking and Pioneering Historical Events*, 2nd ed. Detroit: Visible Ink Press, 2002.

Staniforth, Maxwell, Translator. *Meditations (Penguin Classics) by Marcus Aurelius.* New York: Penguin Classics, 1964.

Sullivan, Otha Richard. *African American Inventors (Black Stars).* San Francisco: Jossey-Bass, 1998.

United States Census Bureau. "Population Estimates: National Characteristics: Vintage 2015." Accessed 2015. http://www.census.gov/popest/data/national/asrh/2015/index.html.

United States Census Bureau. "Black (African-American) History Month: February 2016." Accessed 2016. http://www.census.gov/population/projections/data/national/2014.

U.S. Equal Employment Opportunity Commission. *Job Patterns for Minorities and Women in Private Industry (EEO-1).* Accessed February 29, 2012, from http://www1.eeoc.gov/eeoc/statistics/employment/jobpat-eeo1/2010/index.cfm#select_label.

Whitmore, Roy. *Sam the Sorcerer vs. American Heroes.* Charleston, SC: CreateSpace Independent Publishing Platform, 2012.

Whitmore, Roy. "The Use of Heuristics by Senior Executives when Selecting Senior-Level Executive Direct Reports." PhD dissertation, Fielding

Graduate University, ProQuest, 2013. http://search.proquest.com.fgul. idm.oclc.org/pqdtlocal1006242/docview/1426825660/848E70C9E8F14 38CPQ/1?accountid=10868.

Woodson, Carter Godwin. *The Mis-Education of the Negro*. Las Vegas: Lits, 2010.

Made in the USA
San Bernardino, CA
15 August 2017